PRESERVING OUR WORLD

A Consumer's Guide To The Brundtland Report

by Warner Troyer

Foreword by
Madame Gro Harlem Brundtland

This book is printed on recycled paper

Published by
Warglen International Communications Inc.

Second Printing September 1990

ISBN 0-9694538-1-7

Printed in Canada by Webcom Ltd. Toronto.

Jacket Design by Susan Darrach.

DEDICATION

To Madame Gro Harlem Brundtland
and
To my parents, Ruth and Gordon Troyer
who taught me to care
and to preserve

TABLE OF CONTENTS

Page

Acknowledgements

First, and always, to Madame Gro Harlem Brundtland without whom, ...etc. She has provided inspiration for a generation - and a planet. Her kind and generous comments about this manuscript have been both encouraging and reassuring.

Next to Jim MacNeil, former Executive Director to the UN Commission on Environment and Development. He was kind enough to read the first draft of this manuscript. The 30+ pages of foolscap comment he supplied consequently assisted greatly in avoiding oversimplifications and departures from the spirit of the WCED Report. Neither Madame Brundtland nor Jim McNeil, of course, bear any responsibility for what appears here.

To, also, the Canadian International Development Agency: CIDA funded part of the costs of researching and writing a first draft of this manuscript, through the good offices of Wayne Kynes - a dedicated environmentalist based in Ottawa. And to Wayne, who published an early, edited version of this manuscript in his tabloid publication, "Tribute."

Beyond that, to friend and guru, Stephen Lewis, who alerted me to the WCED Commission and report - and Maurice Strong, who assisted us in getting a pre-publication transcript of the report. Each was more than kind in their "review" of the manuscript. Both men, superb and unequalled world citizens, have served their planet and planetary neighbors far beyond anything my words could express.

To Brenda Ackerman, computer expert par exellence; no one else could have repaired my ten-thumb approach to computer composition.

And to Glenys - partner, colleague, editor, critic, lover, wife. Our arrangement, for fifteen years, has been that she will do the work while I take the credit. Nothing of this - or much else, would have been possible without her support, encouragement, professional skill and intelligence.

Most of this manuscript was written at our cottage on Smoke Lake. It was both the serenity and the natural setting which made this work so integral a part of our lives. Over more than twenty years we've played host to (or been tolerated by) black bear, snapping turtles, mink, otter, lynx, grouse, deer, moose, flying squirrels, owls and myriad birds. Between them, they have brought joy and promise to us and our children, as they do, now, to our grandchildren. Bless them all.

FOREWORD

The Commision's report is a consensus document by commisioners from 21 countries. It is designed to sound an alarm and lay the foundation for debate. I therefore challenge you to test our report. Did we weaken our argument in places by being too general, by not naming names? You name the names.

Unless we are able to translate our words into language that can reach the minds and hearts of people young and old, we shall not be able to undertake the extensive social changes needed to correct the course of development.

It is necessary that the message reach all the citizens of this world. It is a part of the debt we owe them. For our report was written by the people of the world. It is our duty to recycle these findings. And this must be done by you, because the official work of the Commission is over.

You have a reputation for being frank and direct. Put it to good use now.

In the Commission, we have presented a general case for sustainable development. But this is meaningless unless sustainable development is woven into the fabric of all our lives - through individual action, through government policies and laws, and through corporate policies and programmes. Now it is up to you to judge governments and corporations:

Prepare report cards on them. Examine their operations. Measure what governments and private sector groups *say* against what they *do*.

Securing our common future will require new energy, openness to fresh insights. The young are better at such vision than we. We must ask them to monitor our actions, comment on our progress and inform our consciences.

Major changes are crucial. We have the ability to change. We have the technology. We have the communications skills.

The work must begin with individuals, in our homes and villages. We must marshall public will to create political will, reaching to the decision-making chambers of government, to our international institutions and to our transnational boardrooms.

We believe that human resources and ingenuity, our capacity to address the issues in a responsible and concerted manner, have never been greater. We can, together, solve both energy and environmental problems in a new era of economic growth. We face - and must create - an era in which economy and ecology are merged at all levels of decision-making. And there must, to accomplish this, be a more equitable distribution of wealth both within and between nations.

We must accept the fact that environmental considerations are part of a unified management of our planet. This is our ethical challenge. This is our practical challenge. This is a challenge we must all take up.

Securing our common future will require fresh insights. We must develop an ability to look beyond the narrow boundaries of national frontiers or even those of separate scientific disciplines. We must recreate Renaissance thinking

But it begins, it can only begin, with the informed individual and the clarity and vigor of our young people. The young are better at such vision than we who are often constrained by the traditions of a more narrow and fragmented, compartmentalized world. We must tap their energy and their ability to see the interdependence of issues.

All our concerns have come together. Now we know we cannot conserve species when international trade patterns force agricultural nations to destroy natural habitats to plant cash crops. While shipping food and blankets to victims of droughts, famines and floods we must also act against their underlying causes.

Only growth can eliminate poverty. Only growth offers hope for a better life and creates the capacity to solve environmental problems. Human and national inequality is clearly the planet's main environmental problem.

As East and West move from confrontation to cooperation, and as the barriers between us come down, we must build a new coalition of reason. That coalition is essential for our common security and our common survival.

The message of sustainable development is a political necessity and an intellectual imperative. Let us all, sharing insights and informing one another's choices, work together in broadening the options for the present generation and keeping open the options for future generations.

Let no one tell you to "mind your own business". Survival is *everyone's*. business. And the first, vital step is to become an informed participant in our development, an informed and thoughtful partner in our common environment.

It is my hope that the Commission's report, as laid out in this interpretation by Warner Troyer, will assist you in understanding the issues and needs common to everyone on our planet - and move you to participate in the great debate and work toward the global solutions we must all help to develop.

Gro Harlem Brundtland

INTRODUCTION

This modest book celebrates what I believe to be the major causal factor in today's global "green revolution."

There aren't many occasions in human history when we can pin down the precise time and cause of major shifts in public opinion and priorities. The marches in Selma, Alabama were one; Three Mile Island and Chernobyl combined were probably another. The Report of the World Commission On Environment and Development was another. It has already had an impact. Heeded, it could save our planet, our grandchildren, and their grandchildren.

Rachel Carson alerted the world to environmental destruction, in 1962, with her book The Silent Spring. She frightened us, and with cause. More than twenty-five years passed before Madame Gro Harlem Brundtland gave us (in her report, "Our Common Future") cause to restore hope for a safe future with her finely-reasoned analysis of the links between development and environment.

Maybe the most fundamental - and exciting - concept so clearly stated in Our Common Future is that of "sustainable development." Put most simply, Madame Brundtland tells us we cannot find the resources we need to sustain and repair our environment without development - but we can live only with development which can be continued - "sustained" - without environmental damage. So the words to describe "sustainable development" mean precisely what they say: Development our fragile planet can sustain. Without that definition, and that goal, we've no hope.

As a journalist preoccupied both with environmental and Third World issues, I was astonished by the quantum shift in concern for environmental dangers at the end of the Eighties. Sure, most folk had been "concerned" earlier; a substantial fraction of us were even trying to encourage remedies and reduce hazards. Yet when I'd tried to "sell" ideas for environmental stories (to radio, tv, newspapers and magazines) in the late Fifties, Sixties, Seventies and early Eighties, I was frequently told, "I think we did one of those last year. Anyhow, no one is interested." But suddenly, between 1987 and 1989, our global society seemed to develop the critical mass of concern needed to generate virtually perpetual motion in environmental affairs.

In 1970, as producer of a network current affairs television magazine programme, I decided to do an investigative piece on the (frequently unsafe) disposal of industrial toxic waste - from used motor oil to industrial chemicals. We began, in the usual way, by researching the existing literature - newspaper files, libraries, scientific journals et al. In the event, we found two - and only two - very brief stories from the previous decade buried in the New York Times computer. In the end we had, by default, a scoop - because, until then, no one else in North America had been much interested in the subject.

In 1987, in Canada and the United States, one might encounter one environnmental story in a week's tv viewing or newspaper reading; suddenly, by the autumn of 1988, there were many daily stories in all the media.

Our most hidebound politicians, by the winter of 1988/89, were self-inflicting almost visible intellectual hernias in their headlong race to climb aboard the environmental bandwagon.

The "kick-start" for all of this activity was the Report of the World Commission On Environment and Development called, for Commission chairman Gro Harlem Brundtland, the Brundtland Report. Suddenly there was hope we could turn back the tide of pollution smothering the world. Environmental interest, concern and, wonder-of-wonders, action, began to move from the church basements and storefront advocacy groups to the corporate boardrooms. I had a brief, close-up view of one such transformation, in the head offices of one major supermarket chain - the Loblaws company in Toronto - and was (and still am) stunned by the transformation, and the enthusiasm with which environmental responsibility was embraced. Finally, people who, for a generation, had refused to take "yes" for an answer were realizing that good and sound environment practices happened also to be good economics.

Suddenly, everyone was quoting the Brundtland Report (or "Our Common Future," as the published version is titled). But as with those two other revered best sellers, Shakespeare and the Bible, it often seemed there were environmental theologians and scholars appearing everywhere, prepared to interpret a book they hadn't actually read. That's respectable, to a degree:

The Brundtland Report was written for the unanimous consent of Commission members from around the world - from the developed and developing nations, from non-aligned nations as well as those from the East and West Blocs (and this well before the political thaws of 1989/1990). So the Report was couched, in entirely respectable ways and for utterly respectable reasons, in language and terms which could attract consensus from such a disparate group. The miracle was that so varied a group came, through their mutal experience, to full agreement in every area. This triumph of composition, in the best sense and at the highest level of international, world-class, public service prose, was an achievement of unanimous endorsement.

However, for the ordinary reader, that triumph may seem to have come at the expense of human scale and anecdotal example. With only one metaphor in over 140,000 words, and a need to dot every political "i" and cross every potentially disruptive "t," some passages may have seemed somewhat obscure to a casual reader.

The reasoning of the Brundtland Report is stunning and irresistible, and the conclusions tough, dramatic - indeed, revolutionary. But the language of international diplomacy has few adjectives or analogies - nor is it always sympathetic to declarative sentences and simple, direct and unmistakable conclusions.

As will be seen, I suffered from no such constraints. Neither the conclusions nor the recommendations of the WCED Report have been trifled with in what follows. They have, usually, been stripped of some of the excess clauses and sub-clauses which maybe softened the stark realities they observed, judged and reported.

A further personal observation: As a career journalist I have developed a very highly-organized sense of scepticism - not least with regard to pronouncements from politicians and bureaucrats. My professional experience has, over thirty-five years, rarely failed to reinforce and justify that scepticism. So, when I first read an advance copy of the WCED Report text it was with a combined and conflicting sense both of mounting excitement and growing doubt. "I am," I vowed, "going to check this against my own experience in Africa, Asia, Europe, Latin America and North America; I am going to measure it against my professional experience with scientists, researchers, teachers, politicians, manufacturers." I did. And only then was I excited. Gro Brundtland was right, said experience, vetting, scepticism and fear of being led up some new and seductive garden path. It was then - and only then - I determined to, with whatever impertinence, write a more "user friendly" version of the WCED Report in the hope of making it widely accessible to those of us who do not happen to be international bureaucrats or statesmen, career environmentalists or journalists. Just as war is too important to be left to the generals, the book - and our shared environment, was simply too damned important to be left to the "experts," I decided. I hope you will agree.

So what follows is not the Report of the World Commission on Environment and Development. That study is more than three times longer than this compression. So some of the WCED Report's detailed reasoning is missing here, as are some of the "fine print" recommendations. There are additions in this version, as well as deletions:

Extrapolations have been made from WCED data, illustrations have been added, quotations inserted: all of this in an effort to make this arguably most-vital-study-of-the-century clearly relevant and easily understandable.

Some liberties have not been taken. Examples:

-    All the major recommendations of the Brundtland Report are here.

-    Whenever the words, "must," or "should" appear in urging response and action, they are rooted **directly** in the recommendations and convictions of the WCED.

We have the means within us to diagnose our planet's ills -

and the strength, among us, to cure them. What's been lacking is the itinerary - the "Michelin Guide to global survival." The Brundtland Commission has given us that.

What's also been missing is the will to act against the literal "sea of troubles" we face - along with those in our atmosphere, our soil, plants, animals.

We've lacked will partly because we were not prepared to contemplate a downward spiral into "zero growth" - a state of stasis in which more creature comfort, more prosperity and security were unattainable. The WCED Report demonstrates we need fear no such threat. Security, says the Brundtland Report, is possible **only** with growth and development. We can't have security without prosperity.

Beyond that, our concern for environmentally sound development has been hobbled by ignorance. The massive research commissioned, gathered, and brilliantly analyzed by the WCED should end that state of suicidal tunnel-vision. We need, after the Brundtland Report, no longer imitate the self-destructive behaviour patterns sometimes seen in other species with whom we share our tiny, fragile, global village.

An animal, fed a dish which makes it ill, will readily eat the same unsafe food tomorrow; it can't make the connection between something eaten at eight in the morning, and vomiting at noon. So, too, with infants or small children who will, if hungry, scrape the plaster from the wall of a hut (or an inner-city tenement) or eat "mud pies," even feces.

Extrapolation and analysis are impossible without intelligence, a capacity for abstract thought - call it an ability to imagine "what if?" - and experience.

We are supposed to be the one species which can learn from experience. We do extrapolate. Sometimes. Too often not enough, or quickly enough. (If we used our reasoning potential, every tobacco manufacturer would be bankrupt.) Arnold Toynbee said his years of scholarship persuaded him mankind never learned the major lessons of history. The punishment of which we've all been warned is that,

"Those who do not remember the past are condemned to relive it."

That proscription would be bad enough, were it the whole story. It's not. There's been a quantum change in our global village since George Santayana's warning. With our technology, we can create conditions unprecedented in all human history. If we destroy the ozone layer, cause continuing deforestation and desertification, acidify our lakes and forests, poison our ecosphere, there will be no question of our grandchildren being forced to repeat our sad history.

There'll be no environmental resources, no viable ecosphere, left for them to destroy. So we can shorten the rubric, if we refer to current history:

"Those who do not remember the past are condemned." Period.

The Brundtland Report is about connections. With arguments made irresistible by their foundation of massive, meticulous research, the Commission documents and demonstrates the utter madness of viewing the world's myriad problems in isolation. The WCED has made the connections as plain as an anatomy chart. Now we can draft and prove environmental equations showing the links in our chain of global grief. Example:

a)   If industrial nations and banks continue to charge developing nations high interest rates for aid money and development funds, then,

b)   Those Third World nations will have to increase their production of marketable goods to raise hard currency for interest payments, which means,

c) Farmers will over-cultivate even marginal land causing erosion, even desertification leading with stunning speed to,

d) Flooding, drought and the loss of farmland of any value in future as well as,

e)   Much higher rates of hunger and starvation, of waterborne illness which will, in turn,

f)   Quickly make it impossible for poor nations to pay their debts though they will try, not least by,

g)   Diverting funds normally used for education, health, economic development and provision of services to debt payment which will,

h)   Exacerbate the spiral of poverty with all its attendant disasters leading to a situation in which,

i)   The industrial world will have to pour in ever greater amounts of aid to the point at which we may see the entire world economy collapse and, with it,

j)   The remorseless and inexorable destruction of our ecosystem as we scramble ever more frantically to wrest our needs from a bruised and depleted planet.

In making these connections the WCED Report does much more: it tells us we can reverse the equation.

By analyzing the connections we can replace or repair the weak links in the chains binding development to the environment. Instead of the doomsday equation sketched above, we can, literally, "grow our way" to an environmentally stable and prosperous global village. Those poor nations, as we begin to realize, are our neighbours: they can become our partners-in-growth as well.

IF we make the connections.

Not long ago, Sunday School collections for "those poor souls" across the seas were regarded, with considerable and pious pride, as philanthropy. To prove Toynbee wrong, we should draw a lesson from more recent history. The man who wrote the lesson for us was U.S. General George C. Marshall:

May 1945:

Industrial and urban Europe was a charred ruin: Europeans faced starvation; epidemics triggered by the destruction of water and sewerage services; lack of an industrial base; acute shortages of fuel; a monumental shortage of shelter; millions of refugees helpless to return to their own countries and communities, to fend for themselves in any way; hundreds-of-thousands doomed to spend years in "displaced persons' camps" - no one wanted them; schools, where they still stood, closed - and children, in any event, too hungry, too ill-clothed, too apathetic to absorb learning; farmland devastated; and to top it all, Europe's economy paralyzed, with debt to the "New World" it could never hope to repay. Nor could the European states even plan a recovery and development plan:

There were no bootstraps left by which they could pull themselves up.

Enter George C. Marshall, then U.S. Secretary of State, and under his sponsorship, the Marshall Plan for European recovery:

War debts were written-off. Massive aid, in money, goods

and expertise, were funneled into Europe. Huge training schemes were initiated to replace the storehouse of human skills lost in war and universal educational systems were set in place.

The entire continent of Europe had become what we now call a Third World or "Less Developed Nation" to a degree unmatched in any of today's poor countries.

George Marshall rallied the world to change all that. Was it philanthropy? Sure. But looking back from the Eighties, we can discern a large fraction of enlightened self-interest in the recipe:

George Marshall knew there could be no United States as he knew it without access to the resources - the goods and services and talents of Europe - and the markets of a prosperous Europe. He found a way to create the access. **The Marshall Plan was as much a blueprint for the survival of the Americas as for Europe's rebirth.**

Just so is the WCED Report a route map to global survival and prosperity. The analogy with the Marshall Plan is accurate:

The Third World, too, has been devastated by war - not always in the military sense. Some of its historic defeats have been in the battles of commodity trade; in the long retreat from economic stability in the face of overwhelming debt; in the blitzkrieg of drought and illness; in the scorched earth tactics of erosion, deforestation, desertification; in the blockades of clean water, sanitation and immunization; in the torpedoes of Bhopal and the rest; in the massed artillery assaults of pollution; in the hit-and-run raids on non-renewable resources.

There is gallantry, courage and even hope in the Third World: But their troops in this war are best compared to Polish cavalrymen, lances in hand, spurring their horses against Tiger tanks. It's time for a global Marshall Plan.

The entire industrial world now faces the dilemma resolved for the Americas, in 1945, by George Marshall.

What's extraordinary about the Brundtland Report, like the Marshall Plan before it, is its undeniable pragmatism.

What we must now study is the web of connections through which we can protect and preserve our global

village and all who live here with us. The WCED
Report tells us where to begin that odyssey. It is, as
for Dorothy in The Land of Oz, our "yellow brick
road." Along the way, as with her companions, we can
recognize we have the heart, the brains and the
courage needed, even if we've not much used them 'til
now. Read on:

Chapter One

THE THREATS TO
OUR COMMON FUTURE

The topic is, "Environment and Development." So some definitions may be in order. Try this one, from Madame Brundtland:

**THE ENVIRONMENT IS WHERE WE ALL LIVE.
DEVELOPMENT IS WHAT WE ALL DO.**

We are beginning to identify and understand the many individual threats to our environment and, thereby, our survival. Now we know the future of our ecosystem and, ultimately, of our children's lives is inextricably linked to human and economic development at every level. Most of the major individual perils will be examined as we review the Commission's findings: so, too, the connections to the only hope for solutions - the careful and deliberate use of rational and sustainable development as a tool to save our global village.

The possibility of failure is entirely real. The time frame within which we can ensure survival is short.

-    We have already lost millions of hectares of arable land. **Every year**, we permanently lose six million more hectares of farmland to our mushrooming deserts. Put it this way: six million hectares equal 23,156 square miles; that is more than four times the entire area of Jamaica or three times the size of Israel. We "grow" more desert, desert we may never reclaim, than the land area of Austria or Belgium every eighteen months; an area greater than Denmark each thirty weeks; consider all of Greece laid waste in just two years; all of Japan reduced to sand and rock in six years; the entire United Kingdom as sterile as the moon in just four years. The problem is not modest.

1

-    Many species of both plants and animals are extinct - we killed them. In Western Equador alone, where forests have been destroyed to establish banana plantations, as many as 50,000 different animal species were utterly destroyed in just the period from 1960 to 1985! We are now destroying three more species every day. By the end of the decade it will be three species lost every hour.

-    Even among the living, tens-of-millions of children and adults, their minds and bodies stunted by malnourishment in infancy, have been permanently robbed of the possibility of ever becoming full and contributing members of society.

-    As a direct result of vitamin 'A' deficiency, a half-million children are blinded, in the developing world, each twelve months. Every ten years, to put the numbers in context, our global village has a new sub-stratum of permanently blind kids more than large enough to populate all of Berlin, Caracas, Boston, Rome, Sydney or Athens. One more child, blind, in the sixty-or-so seconds it has taken you to read this paragraph; and in the Third World, with few centres for rehabilitation and vocational training, each of these kids will be a drain on their family and on society, not a participant in or contributor to development.

For those kids, for the now-extinct animal species, the ravaged farmland forever deprived of its food production potential, any "window-of-opportunity" has passed. Those random examples are grim but salient.

One threat over-rides all others: the possibility, writ large by our current behaviour, the global village may fail to act in concert.

Madame Brundtland expressed the danger best:

The earth is one; but the world is not.

We mostly seek our own individual, national, at best regional goals with little regard for the consequences of our acts on other people and countries. We must get together, or fall apart. The Brundtland Report shows us we can "Preserve Our World."

The best evidence of our capacity to endure, to ensure survival, lies in our recent history. We have made progress; we can fashion broad, strategic goals and work in unison to achieve them:

-   The "killer smogs" are no more in London; there are edible fish, again, in the Thames.

-   The industrial nations are taking the lead out of gasoline, and paint.

-   We have mostly stopped using the phosphate detergents which were choking our waterways less than two decades ago.

-   In the time since 1950, in the developing world, the percentage of children dying before age five has been reduced by half.

-   Over the past thirty-five years, human life expectancy in our global village has risen a dramatic thirty percent-plus - from forty-six years to sixty-one.

-   In 1970, just thirteen of every hundred rural families in the Third World had access to safe drinking water; today the proportion is forty-four percent.

-   Adult literacy, world-wide, has rocketed to seventy-two percent from fifty-five percent, in thirty-six years.

-   In the Third World, in 1946, fewer than half of all children even started school; now ninety-five percent at least begin.

-   In 1970, only one-in-twenty of the globe's kids had been immunized; today we treat four-in-ten.

Still, there's no time for the luxury of self-congratulation just yet. The equally devastating time bombs of growing poverty and the narrow-focused pursuit of short-term prosperity-at-any-cost are still with us; their fuses are not very long; and they are linked.

Our best hope is in the growing, global constituency-of-concern. We cannot move effectively without universal, public demand and support. "Public will" soon translates into "political will" in any culture or nation state. But public will, uninformed, is impotent at best - dangerous at worst. So we must identify the enemy, the causes of our jeopardy; each leaves its own unique fingerprints on the ecological systems of destruction we witness. Tracing our vulnerabilities from symptoms to causes, we may then seek the new approaches needed to cure the disease. Let's begin with a brief overview of those symptoms and their causes:

What's Happening To Us - and Why:

We generally measure or identify damage to our global village by noting, even quantifying, what is called, "environmental stress." The term is a handy grab-all phrase or shorthand, but with strong overtones of Orwellian "Newspeak." Like many specially coined contemporary phrases it seems designed more to lull anxiety than to heighten awareness. (One is reminded of the Canadian Air Force manual description of, "helmets, anti-buffeting" in place of "crash helmets".) Similarly, "environmental stress" covers a multitude of horrors, from dead lakes and extinct species to mass starvation, moribund national economies and the steadily increasing migration of literally millions of refugees.

If anyone speaks of environmental problems we look to over-use of resources and pollution as the chief villains. There is another:

Poverty may be the greatest single enemy of our environment. The poor and the hungry destroy their own environment, and another fraction of the globe's capacity for survival, in efforts to stay alive one more day or year. Forests are cut for the income from timber, and to open more land, often marginal land, to farming. Grasslands are over-grazed. Hillsides are stripped and cultivated, causing erosion and the permanent loss of any thin mantle of topsoil. When the land is exhausted, these folk migrate to the cities in a crushing human wave which can neither be employed nor provided the basic needs of survival by overburdened municipalities.

None of this is to suggest untramelled development is the best way to solve the problems of poverty. The indiscriminate use of resources, chemicals, energy, petroleum-based synthetics is as real a danger as we've imagined.

A key to the hazards of the "instant gratification" system of industrial development lies in the infantile misapplication of economic goals and principles.

Environmental costs must be a part of any cost/benefit

analysis, whether in banking procedures, plant construction or commodities distribution.

It's a truism in industry that "retro-fits" are, literally, forty times more costly, on average, than solutions built into original design. Small wonder, when the usual lead time for a new industrial product is about seven years. (There must be market surveys; analyses of the availability of labour, material and other resources; an examination of competition; the search for capital; the design of product; the construction of plant; the training of personnel; the development of quality control standards; the commissioning of packaging, advertising and market strategies; the guarantee, contractually, of materials and parts at economic rates; the forecasts needed to estimate the impact of taxation, tariffs, transportation costs; and so on, and on.) It's during this long phase the environmental "bugs" must be identified and eliminated. To do a "quick fix" when they're found, later, (as surely they will be) isn't quick at all; and the "fixes", as we've noted, cost forty times and more than would have been the case if they'd been included in the basic design. **Crisis management, it turns out, is profoundly bad economics.**

Preventive strategies are the only ones which make economic (as well as environmental) sense.

Increasingly, polluters are getting caught, and being forced to repair the damage, modify the fault in their process or product. The environmental lawsuits of the past decade are sufficient evidence of the lousy economics of pollution, to say nothing of the monumental sums needed to modify faulty systems. (Ask any auto manufacturer the cost of a single "recall.")

So the battle for survival in our global village has two enemies, two targets which we once supposed were unrelated:

The first is lack of sufficient development; call it poverty, for its symptom.

The second is mindless development; call it pollution, for its symptom.

Both are economically untenable and unsustainable. We are beginning to realize they are fatal, in both environmental and human terms. But the third factor in the equation-of-survival (or conversely, the equation-of-disaster) is economic; and it's this recognition which gives us the understanding we need to save ourselves and our fragile planet.

Let's look first at the consequences of poverty.

We should begin by understanding the failure of some traditional forms of foreign aid to solve the riddles of poverty. As with industrial retro-fits, much of our aid money goes for crisis management. That's essential in times of flood, famine, and natural disaster but useless with regard to eliminating global poverty. Some perspective:

Proportionately fewer of the world's population go hungry now than in 1970. But in absolute numbers, more people are so short of food they suffer permanent physical stunting and brain damage. This, of course, because of our global population increase.

We aren't keeping up.

Similarly, while the percentage of Third World families with access to safe drinking water is up, with our rising global population, the total number of people who have no access to the "health insurance" afforded by clean water is up, too.

Urban migration has enormously swelled the numbers (well into their tens-of-millions, now) of slum and shanty town dwellers in the developing world; they live in cardboard or palm thatch shacks, in sewer culverts and ditches.

Consider the most pragmatic consequences of enduring and escalating poverty:

First, as we know, the poor are a back-breaking burden for any but the richest of societies. The provision of services to the poor - from food, health care, shelter and energy to education is beyond the capacity of most developing nations. Look at just one facet of the evidence, the world simply "can't afford poverty": Examples:

a) In various Third World nations, from twenty-five to seventy percent of all hospital beds are occupied by patients suffering from water-borne or water-related disease.

b) At the same time, from fifty to sixty percent of **all** health care costs in developing countries are directly triggered by unclean water.

But the World Health Organization calculates these nations would recoup the entire cost of providing safe water for every citizen on earth, in from five to ten years, in reduced health and hospital costs. Surely an amortization plan like that would satisfy the most hard-headed business or industrial economist. There's more:

a) Ten million of our neighbours in the global village die, each year, of water-borne disease. (Call that the combined populations of Rio de Janeiro and Beijing wiped-out, every year; every three years, as many deaths as in World War Two.)

b) If they lived, each of those individuals, as adults, would contribute maybe $50 annually, in direct and indirect taxes, to their societies. (Aggregate taxes, worldwide, vary from thirty to seventy percent of gross national product; the figure for Canada, for example, is now over fifty percent. And even the poorest of Third World nations have a per capita GNP near $200 U.S.) Over a lifetime of earnings, each of those folk would, therefore, have added at least $2,000 to the tax revenues of their communities - money available for services and development.

c) Each such individual, in the poorest nation on earth, would contribute at least four times more, say eight thousand dollars, to their nation's GNP over a lifetime of work.

Now consider the purely economic loss to us all of our failure to provide clean drinking water to the Third World:

With ten million slain by impure water this year, our global village has lost $20 billion in future tax revenue, and $80 billion in future GNP. We'll suffer the same loss, every year, until we spend just five percent of the annual loss on development - according to WHO estimates - to provide safe drinking water for every man, woman and child on the planet.

Poverty is rotten economics.

Human costs aside, here's one more example of how poverty exacts huge costs from everyone in the world, and directly, not just those in the poor nations:

As we've noted, the poor over-cultivate their land, eliminate their forests, denude their slopes and hills. They also settle on and farm any available land: in river valleys prone to flooding, on unprotected coastal plains. The result is not just soil erosion or even desertification:

In the Sixties, 5.2 million people were flood victims. In the Seventies, floods claimed 15.4 million victims. When the figures are all in for the Eighties, they will be higher still.

During the Seventies, six times as many people died from "natural disasters," every year, as in the Sixties. The figures for the Eighties will almost certainly add to the exponential curve of tragedy.

WHY?

Not because of angry gods or sunspots. Most of these were not "natural disasters" at all:

Look instead to high interest charges on Third World debt, to declining world commodity prices, as a **direct cause** of those disasters. In Bangladesh, as an example, flooding has been linked, directly, to erosion caused by over-cutting of forests. But the forests were over cut to earn the short-term, foreign exchange cash needed to compensate for lower commodity income and higher debt costs. Then consider the nearly incalculable cost to the industrial states, in emergency aid, to succor those struck by drought, flood, famine, epidemic.

Western governments, fearful of the political consequences of their own national deficits, might look to the vast sums squandered on poverty. The global village is, indeed, living beyond its means. The luxury we can no longer afford is world poverty.

Poverty burns the heart and substance out of any society it strikes as surely as an out-of-control forest fire. We have to recognize, now, there are no international "fire breaks" we can build to protect the industrial world from the conflagration raging in the Third World. Economic and ecological hazards and disasters have long since stopped being contained by any man-made frontier. "One planet" it has always been. "One world" it is, for us to share, or to destroy.

Our problems stem, as I hope we've now seen and agreed, from insufficient development (or poverty, in shorthand), and indiscriminate development (shorthand: pollution). Let's look at the second of the horns of our dilemma:

We are growing, globally, almost like Alice after she quaffed the, "drink me" potion in Wonderland. Consider:

a)   Annual fossil fuel use has increased thirty times in the past century. Three-quarters of this increase occurred after World War Two.

b)   Industrial production is up to fifty times its level of a century ago. Eighty percent of that expansion has been since 1950.

c)   We've cleared more land for human settlement and agriculture in this century than in all of recorded human history combined.

The benefits of expansion are clear: better health; longer life expectancy; universal education; better shelter; higher living standards and a decent "quality of life" - but only for those of us who share in prosperity. Growth can skew consumption and, thereby, the availability of resources needed for survival. Some quick examples:

Consumers in the industrial nations use 160 times more energy, per person, than those in the developing states.

We use ten times more paper products.

We consume 50 percent more calories, daily, 100 percent more protein, and 110 percent more fat.

We use thirty times more water, per capita.

The industrial nations, per capita, use fifteen times more steel and a thirteen times disproportionate share of other metals.

Not much room, there, for the Third World to catch-up.

Modern technology has helped industrial nations reduce resource consumption (especially in the field of energy) while maintaining, even increasing, productivity. In Japan since the "oil crunch" of 1973, the amount of energy and raw materials used in industry for each unit of production from a pocket calculator to a TV set, a computer or an automobile, **has been reduced by sixty percent.** But rising incomes - and populations - in developing nations will keep the pressure on finite resources.

Our survival demands we learn to understand the fragile connections between our global resources. There are some thresholds we mustn't cross in our race to develop new

9

products, accelerate growth, increase prosperity. The overall fabric of our ecosphere can, we know now, be damaged beyond repair by unthinking activity in just one area. Each segment of our ecosphere is linked to all others, as surely as the compartments of a submarine. Damage the watertight integrity of the submarine in one - punch one hole in the hull, and everyone drowns. That "multiplier effect" is as real on the surface of our planet. Example:

The "greenhouse effect" caused by burning fossil fuels which create an accumulation of carbon dioxide in the atmosphere leads directly to environmental degradation and, in turn, to even more poverty, with the spiraling consequences we've examined.

We can no more play Russian roulette with our planet. Nor will there be any use, when the wounds are fatal, murmuring "we didn't know the gun was loaded."

It may already be too late to repair the hole in the ozone layer over the Antarctic caused in part by CFCs from degrading foam plastic containers, escaping gas from air conditioners and "spray can" aerosol emissions. Already, ozone depletion has led to an extra 100,000 new cases of blindness from cataracts, worldwide, every year. Moreover, every one percent decrease in the ozone layer leads directly to a three percent increase in skin cancer.

Acid rain can do far more than end trout fishing in tourist areas: the loss of whole forests means more soil erosion, more climatic change and, long term, more flooding, siltation and the rest. **The American Medical Association now ranks acid rain as the second leading cause of lung cancer, after smoking; and World Health officials believe acid rain may be responsible for a global doubling of deaths from asthma over the past decade.**

Our disposal of toxic wastes - more accurately, our failure to safely dispose of toxic wastes - means we are leaving a lethal promissory note for future generations. Some "experts" of this generation may regard the risks of accumulating radioactive wastes as "acceptable." **They** will not bear the risks of these poisons, poisons which will be active for centuries; it will be their descendants who learn whether our gamble - on their lives - was justified. **They** have not been consulted.

Just as we are "willing" those hazards we've created to children not yet born, we are also "exporting" hazards without the consent or knowledge of our neighbours in the global village. The movements of man-made poisons through our air and water have made pollution the globe's leading trans-national activity.

What must concern us most is our ignorance. We simply do not know when some of our crimes-of-omission will cause environmental degradation to snowball into a critical mass, a chain reaction beyond our control. No scientist can say when we'll cross a final threshold, when the greenhouse effect will cause climatic changes sufficient to destroy civilization as we know it.

We do know time is short. The global survival clock, however out of focus for us, is surely in its last hour.

So more research, more study, more analysis and understanding are essential. But we need not have any more information to begin acting in our own interest. When a child has pneumonia, we don't decide "more research is needed" before giving antibiotics and oxygen. When floods threaten our homes we don't go off to design a hydro-diversion scheme before we build the sandbag barriers to hold back the water. Of course we want the research to prevent future pneumonia; certainly we want a deeper river channel or diversionary canal to prevent next year's flood. First, though, let's keep that child alive and that home standing.

We know enough now to stop much of the mounting danger and remedy much of the damage already done. To avoid mobilizing the knowledge and skills we have would constitute a kind of global, environmental murder-by-default. Asking for yet more studies before we act is about as sensible as doing a thesis on muzzle velocity and ballistic trajectory while standing in front of a pistol which is about to be fired.

No search for a secure future can have meaning, it must be added, without an infinitely more vigorous and universal effort to end the greatest and most final of all environmental "hazards": the real and persistent possibility of nuclear annihilation.

None of these concerns can be addressed without tackling and overcoming the economic crisis which will otherwise make any progress impossible. High international interest rates, falling prices for Third World goods and higher energy costs can destroy any nation's best efforts to sustain even minimal standards and services. Between 1980 and 1984 alone, for example, plummeting commodity prices cost developing nations $55 billion in lost earnings; and this while debt servicing costs (rising interest rates) were making draconian cuts in available resources. As a direct result, virtually every developing nation (excluding India and China) experienced a drop in GNP in those years.

Nor is the cost of the world economic crisis being shared either with justice or logic. The poor of our global village are bearing the heaviest burden; their consequent over-exploitation of already meagre resources for short-term survival will leave us all poorer. We must revitalize the waning enthusiasm for international and multilateral cooperation. Recent trends to protectionism, trade wars and unilateral fiat can only hurt us all.

The only sensibly selfish attitude remaining to us requires we extend the "self" in that word to all humankind.

In the past we have relied on ingenuity and technical innovation to solve our problems. They are no longer enough. Our ad hoc approach had more to do with tinkering than fixing or curing. Without a holistic approach to environment and development we've no hope of success (for "success," read "survival.") Trying to deal with acid rain, for example, while ignoring the global financial crisis would make about as much sense as bandaging a blistered foot while ignoring a maniac cutting our throat.

All of those "environment stresses" are linked, interconnected. Moreover, the indivisible fabric of environmental hazards is linked just as surely to economic circumstances and development. Energy policies relate directly to the greenhouse effect, to acidification, often to the disruption of wildlife habitat and the flooding of arable land; world trade in agriculture has a direct impact on the degradation of water, soil and forest.

All of those environmental stresses threaten the economic

development we need to build a healthy global village. Equally, mindless (call it "unsustainable") economic development only increases environmental strains.

There are more links, building our three-dimensional model-of-concern: both environmental and economic concerns are directly influenced, every day, by political and social policy. Rapid increase in population, for example, has profound environmental and economic impact. National, political policies directly influence both as well, as is obvious.

And these are all two-way streets: the consequence of environmental stress or uneven economic development will always influence political and social stability. Without improving the lot of the world's women, protecting the vulnerable in our global village, building mechanisms for local involvement in decision-making, there will be no stability for us - not in terms of the environment, of development, or even socially and politically.

We can maybe split the atom or even some of its parts, but the undeniably obvious systemic nature of environment/development/ society/body-politic can be ignored only at a cost beyond our means. These four, as surely as the "air, water, earth and fire" of our forebears are the essential, interdependent forces governing our destiny and survival. They are, literally, symbiotic. If we can understand and manage them for our mutual benefit they can be synergistic. But the "we" in that last sentence is a very large one indeed:

Just as we have separated, balkanized and compartmented our problems in the past, we've isolated and fragmented the assignment of responsibility, and with equal futility. Those environmental ministries and institutions we've expected to protect us have had no control over the processes they were assigned to monitor. Environmental protection, even within a single government, is a lottery when it depends on whether the environment minister has as much cabinet clout as his or her colleagues in energy, agriculture, finance, forestries and the rest. (Canada's government is a depressing study in these terms, as is that of the U.S.) So environment ministers have mostly had to concern themselves with reactive rather than proactive policy; they've become fire-fighters, hosing down blazes which could have been prevented if they'd been permitted to require fireproof building materials, sprinklers, smoke alarms and the rest. The watch-words have been "reforestion" instead of aforestation, "urban renewal" instead of urban planning, "restoration" of natural habitat instead of protection. Instead of being the designers and engineers of a stronger economy and environment, we more nearly resemble that small Dutch boy with his finger in the dike, trying to keep out the North Sea.

To change the system for our benefit, begin with the simplest of realizations:

SURVIVAL IS EVERYBODY'S BUSINESS.

So every ministry must make the environment - the need for environmentally-sustainable development - a primary goal: Indeed, **the** primary goal. So too with every industry, business, economist, and yes, every family and individual.

Treating symptoms won't be enough, anymore: when the pain-killers are no longer effective, there may not be time enough left to ask why we failed to eliminate the illness.

Economists and bankers have to start talking to farmers and primary producers. We can't dump surplus or subsidized agricultural products on any world market, for example, while expecting the Third World to repay foreign debt in a world community where they can no longer compete with **their** products.

Nor can we go on signing the names of our children, and their children, to environmental and developmental I.O.U.s: Especially not when we are, at the same time, spending their birthright of resources at a rate designed to leave them environmentally bankrupt.

Every nation will have to develop policies and procedures appropriate to its unique needs and aspirations. But if all are not coordinated into a global strategy there can be no enduring stability anywhere.

We have to incorporate the democratic principle of "consent" in all of our international mechanisms and agreements: That means "consent" in its full sense - "informed consent."

In medieval times, most communities had a "common," a meadow or square where everyone's livestock grazed, where

14

all members of the community shared a resource and a responsibility. Today that "common" spans the globe. It's not too late to save the "Global Common." If we share the concern and the responsibility, we may also live to share the hope and the rewards.

Chapter Two

DEVELOPMENT WE CAN LIVE WITH

We must, we know, develop to survive. As we've seen, the impact of development is trans-national. More than that, it is trans-generational as well. So the "we" in this chapter's title implies those children yet unborn as well as those of us already here. "Development We Can Live With" must mean:

a) Development which meets the needs of the present and, equally,

b) Development which does not rob future generations of their opportunity to survive and prosper.

There must be equity between generations as well as between and within societies and nations.

Development has no definition in a social vacuum. It has meaning only if and as it serves human needs and aspirations. So to decide what development we want, and how much, we have to refer to the twin criteria which can, alone, justify our plans for growth:

1. What do we need?

2. What limitations must we recognize in deciding what we want and need?

We have some basic guidelines:

We "need" enough development to eradicate global poverty. It's clear we cannot preserve our environment unless we achieve that goal.

We "need" enough development to provide nourishment, shelter, education, employment to all the citizens of our global village.

We "need" enough development to preserve hope.

The obvious limitations we must analyze are equally clear:

We are limited by acts which will destroy any sector of our fragile and interconnected ecosphere.

We are limited by available natural resources.

We are limited by technological state-of-the-art.

Most profoundly, we are limited by a lack of social organization within our global village. We are and will continue to be environmental and developmental paralytics until the public/political will and coordination mechanisms are in place. But we have learned "growth" and "development" are not four-letter words: not if we can live with them. Call that "sustainable development": development that is, and as we've agreed (if you accept what's gone before), within the limits imposed by the simple, direct need for self-preservation. So we have to examine the dimensions and boundaries of our "envelope of freedom" to grow and to act.

U.S. Supreme Court Justice Oliver Wendell Holmes was once required to rule on a civil suit in which one man sued another who had broken his nose at a baseball game. The defendant said he had only been exercising his right to swing his arms in excitement during a critical play. Said Holmes,

"Every man has a right to swing his arms. But that right is circumscribed by the proximity of his neighbour's nose."

We've already bloodied too many noses in our rush to have bigger autos, more comfort, higher incomes. Living on the surface of this time machine called earth, we now risk breaking noses well into the next century.

To meet the needs of our global village, the achievement of our full growth potential is crucial, within the limits we've discussed. Coupled with this is the absolute need to realize an equally full potential in the distribution of resources. We've already accomplished miracles of growth:

- World cereal production has increased 250 percent since 1950.

- Industrial production has been multiplied forty times in thirty-five years.

- Gross world production is up more than twenty-fold since the turn of this century.

At the same time, the gap between rich and poor has widened. "Progress" and "prosperity" have been the preserve, increasingly, of a minority of us. Saying miraculously high production can coexist with widespread poverty is no theory; it is the pervasive fact of this century.

It's time to turn our mastery of natural systems to the common good, the preservation of that "global common" we identified earlier:

Human societies have been "intervening" and "interfering" with the natural-order-of-things for at least ten thousand years. The process began when we first gave up nomadic life for settled, cultivated, agricultural communities. Today the descendants of those first folk to tinker with nature can use nuclear physics to transmute lead into gold, or genetics to create entirely new life forms. King Canute was born too soon.

In China today the sea literally is "held back" from vast tracts of reclaimed land by man-made stone dikes. So what must we do to ensure development-we-can-live-with, sustainable development, and ensure, as critically, equity in the future distribution of benefits from new development?

Some quick answers are easy to describe, if harder to implement:

- Education
- Environmental regulation, inspection and enforcement.
- The creation of institutions to research, design, organize and coordinate environmentally-sound development.

A more difficult goal:

Those effected by environmental hazards must be empowered to influence the events leading to their distress. We all know countless examples of the ways individuals, communities, whole nations and regions are afflicted with environmental damage over which they have no control:

- If farmers take more than their share of irrigation water, the crops of the small-holder downstream won't grow.
- Hot water discharged from a thermal nuclear plant may destroy the livelihood of hundreds of fishermen whose potential catch has been killed.
- Construction of a new highway may expose all the children living near it to lead poisoning from passing traffic.
- Careless use of agricultural pesticides may poison the wells of neighbours through contaminated ground water; and **there is no technology to purify contaminated ground water.**
- An economic decision to reduce hydro costs by burning

cheaper coal in generating stations in one country may multiply acid rain to the point of destroying a forest industry in another, thousands of kilometres distant.

All our social conventions are based on the assumption most of us will respect laws and borders. We have difficulty coping with outlaws. But pollution and environmental degradation are international outlaws. They recognize no rules or international boundaries; they neither carry nor recognize any national flag. No science fiction writer ever invented an enemy more pervasive:

Like some ghostly, time-travelling starship, pollution is able, invisibly, to circle the globe, and extend its destruction throughout whatever remains of human history - into the next century and beyond. So we need new institutions, new tools and weapons to combat a threat which can now cross the boundaries of time as well as space.

The beginnings must be made with the smallest unit - the individual. Yet few of us are willing to initiate change unless we feel our neighbours will do the same. Until we reassure one another we will act responsibly, most of us will go on basing our plans on narrow self-interest. So education is the beginning - in the broadest sense.

(Law, for example, can have an educative element: witness the changes in the use of auto seat belts; think of the improvement in behaviour toward minorities as human rights laws have been adopted in industrial nations. New laws have made some forms of behaviour socially unacceptable. Regulation **does** work as a social inhibitor, not just from fear of penalty, but from knowledge the majority of our peers disapprove. We don't want to be embarrassed by being seen to be out-of-step: fewer people inflict their "sidestream" tobacco smoke on others anymore; fewer drive after drinking alcohol. Both regulation and public education campaigns are effective.)

The trans-national nature of pollution in all its forms adds a new dimension to the problem of regulation. Canada can't regulate acid rain emissions in the United States. Tahiti can't legislate a stop to ocean oil spills which may pollute its beaches and destroy bird and plant life. Argentina can't control interest rates in Germany or Britain which may cripple its ability to provide for its people. Malaysia can't dictate the price of tin in France, nor India the price of tea in Holland.

Bluntly put: no one nation can any longer control or protect its own economy or environment unilaterally. Sweden could not have prevented Chernobyl, though it suffered the consequences. There are, today, two thousand river basins and bodies of seawater contaminated by the ships and industrial emissions, not of the countries adjacent to them, but of a hundred other nations.

The only cure lies in our urgent recognition of common interest in survival. An important first step, having recognized our interdependence, will be to embrace it - to distribute economic decision-making power and trade policy clout more widely. The closer our embrace, the more we will feel moved to cooperate, and confident our efforts will be attended-to and effectual. We can scarcely expect those not invited to the party to help pay for the entertainment.

Cooperation, if we want it, must come soon. The more threadbare our environment, the greater the gaps, and the resentments, between rich and poor. Poor farmers suffer first and most as land deteriorates; they can't afford anti-erosion measures. When mineral resources are depleted, those last at table - the newly-industrializing, developing nations - endure the greatest hardship: they have no stockpiles, no guaranteed supplies. When urban air quality is threatened, the poor (they live in the industrial belts, near the factories where they work, and beside the rail lines) are the first to suffer. But the wealthier folk in industry-free suburbs, on the airy hills, will suffer, too, in time. It would serve those wealthy families and nations best to witness the examples of potential disaster already evident in the neighbourhoods of their less prosperous peers and nations.

One hundred years ago, coal miners carried canaries into the pits with them. If a canary lost consciousness, the miners knew there was gas in the tunnel and they got out, if they could. The industrial nations, however innocently, have been using the developing world as a global pit canary. It's time we recognized the danger signals we've been getting.

The global village is no Welsh coal mine. We can't leave

the canary and run for the surface. So we'd best clear away the gas.

An essential first step will be both to increase and to redistribute income in the Third World. If absolute poverty is not eliminated there's little hope, as we've seen, of preserving the global environment or economy. The task is less Herculean than it might seem. It's estimated extreme poverty in the developing world, where it affects maybe half the total population, could be reduced to a scourge afflicting ten percent of those people, with an annual per capita increase in income of just three percent. (Compare that figure with the most recent set of corporate, executive salaries or collective bargaining agreements of which you've read.) Given population statistics and projections, that would mean an increase in GNP of from five to six per cent in Africa, Asia and Latin America. Possible? Yes!

Research indicates a five percent increase in GNP is realistically attainable in most Asian countries, including India and China. Latin America had growth rates of five percent in the Sixties and Seventies; they were ended by the international debt crisis. An increase of this order will need more difficult structural change in Africa. Moreover, those improvements won't just happen; it will take a global effort. But necessity is a great spur. As Sam Johnson observed:

> "Depend upon it, sir: When a man knows he is to be hanged in a fortnight, it concentrates his mind wonderfully."

In hard truth, with regard to the rigid laws which govern the environment/development equation, we are all in the Third World. It's a very small lifeboat and we'd better all be prepared to bail.

So. Global economic equity is a prerequisite. So is equity within individual nations. Example:

In most Third World nations, income distribution is about like this:

The top one-fifth of households have fifty percent of national income; the bottom fifty percent of families have only about fifteen percent. So, if these ratios are unchanged, overall national income would have to double, to reduce the fraction of families below the poverty line from fifty percent to ten percent.

However, if just twenty-five percent of new income were diverted to those below the poverty line, a mere five percent annual increase in GNP would achieve the same effect within a generation.

In seeking higher incomes for the Third World, as well as greater productivity in the industrial west, the key to survival lies in monitoring the quality of growth.

Industrial nations have learned to produce more, with less energy; with better management of resources; even by recycling material which formerly added to our stockpile of pollutants and toxins. In most industrial countries, to whatever extent, we are turning garbage into energy, manure into biogas, waste petroleum sludge into fuel oil. We must find ways to enlarge these areas of expertise, and to transfer these skills to the Third World.

To control the "quality of growth" we must also begin adding all the factors to our development balance sheets. No industrial economist's spread sheets which ignore potential environment deficits are complete. Economists or industrial planners who regard sound ecological planning as bad business, or irrelevant to their futures, belong on the same scrap heap of history as those who claimed smoking was good for one's health, and rhinoceros horn would improve the libido.

The ancient Greeks had a word for it:

The words "ecology" and "economics" spring from the same Greek root - "eco." The Greek "eco" described either a house or the management and stewardship of a household. Stewardship is a fair description of the task we face in our global household; we'll need total understanding of both ecology and economics to meet that challenge.

In considering both the quality of growth and the potential for it, people must always be seen as the centre of our environment. Healthy, literate people are the yeast of all development, the essential ingredient. Unhealthy, illiterate, hungry people are the greatest obstacle to our survival.

The most basic of all human needs is the means of earning a livelihood; that's fundamental to the others - food, shelter, clothing. By the year 2000 we will have 900 million more people in the global village job market; jobs will have to be found for 60 million of them, every year. If they have jobs, they will be on their way to proper nourishment for themselves and their families. No mean task that:

If our neighbours in the developing world are to eat as well as those in industrial countries by the year 2000, it will take:

Annual increases in consumption, in Africa, of five percent in calories and 5.8 percent in protein.

Increases of three to four percent in Asia and Latin America.

To achieve these goals, considerable increases in protein production will be needed, whether from the cultivation of pulses and oil seeds, the development of dairy industries, the establishment of family "fish farm" ponds or whatever.

Energy availability, too, will be critical. As many as three billion people may live in areas with little or no fuelwood by the end of the century. Alternate fuel and energy sources must be found and made available. Solutions will range from the fuel-efficient, hand-made, clay "Hyderabad stove" to the potential use of super conductors to distribute hydro power.

Population stabilization is a major goal if we are to manage our ecosystem rationally. Ironically, children born in the industrial world impose a far greater burden on the environment through their vastly disproportionate use of resources. But while the industrial world's population will rise only from 1.2 billion to 1.4 billion by 2000, Third World populations will almost double, from 3.7 billion to 6.8 billion. The processes which reduced birth rates in western nations - increased prosperity, economic and social development (including education) are at work in the Third World - but not quickly enough.

Exploding urbanization is equally critical in developing nations. Nearly ninety per cent of Third World population increase will be in the cities; and the cities cannot serve their existing populations. Smaller, satellite cities must be planned. Rural families must be encouraged to stay on the land in the only way practical - by making their lives rewarding.

The continuing pressure on our finite resources and the

over-use of our renewable resources can only delay Third World development. People without alternatives don't look to the future when their bellies are empty today. So Asian fishermen increase their catch by using dynamite, and thereby foreclose next year's fish harvest potential. If their fair share of profits wasn't pre-empted by middlemen and distributors, or shrunk by world commodity price wars, they might be able to resume normal fishing practice and husband their only income resource.

Above all, the industrial nations must help the Third World avoid the dangerous mistakes of western industrialization. We'd have virtually no resources at all if developing nations squandered water, energy, food and the rest with the same profligacy inflicted on our planet by the the West over the last half-century. We must undertake major research aimed at adapting materials technology, energy conservation, biotechnology and the other recent industrial state innovations to Third World needs. We must, too, concentrate more on "social products":

Begin with clean air and water; then consider longer product life and more uniformity of products and parts. We can't afford "planned obsolescence" with our shrinking resources; nor the irrationality of enormous resources used to design and produce parts for products which are "unique" (and useless as replacements excepting in a particular brand and model of auto, razor, refrigerator). Nor should we allocate vast resources dedicated to designing a fancier way of wrapping cigarettes, or designing and building machines with the sole function of packaging a candy-striped toothpaste. "New and better" usually means "more expensive and resource wasteful."

We need, too, to anticipate and plan ahead for ecological risks and hazards. "Risk analysis" is crucial if we are not to rely on spasm response and ad hoc crisis management when there is a Bhopal, a Chernobyl, a Three Mile Island, a Rhine River, a Love Canal. This implies a trans-industry, a trans-sectoral and trans-governmental system of coordination to assess and minimize risks: this because, while several individual industries may each operate within the letter of environmental regulation, the combined impact of their activities may be deadly. Add lead fumes from autos to acid rain from industry and the "multiplier effect" may be fatal.

We can no longer settle for "adequate" limits for individual ecological hazards. Their total, synergistic impact is what matters. The grieving mother of a dead child won't be comforted by the knowledge the amounts of mercury, cadmium, lead, PCBs, pesticide and dioxin ingested were each at a "safe level" if the aggregate witches' brew was lethal.

We will have to change the laws. But without informed and active community participation, world wide, regulation alone is toothless. Resource management must be decentralized, and the public encouraged to participate at all levels of decision-making.

All the components of growth and development policy must be measured against environmental need:

Tax laws, resource development schemes, industrial expansion plans, trade programmes, agricultural subsidies, investment programmes, energy developments: All must meet environmental criteria nationally and internationally.

In many areas of society we have agreed the "innocent until proved guilty" philosophy is inadequate to insure public safety. In these areas of so-called "onus legislation" the accused must prove themselves innocent. So, for example, we must demonstrate we have a valid driver's permit; new patent drugs must be proved safe before they are marketed; food products must be proved to be free of contamination. Perhaps it's time for "onus legislation" in our total environment, rather than just on our highways, in our pharmacies and in our grocery stores. Allowing a "presumption of innocence" and a "benefit of the doubt" to deadly chemicals does justice neither to their distributors and manufacturers nor to the involuntary consumer, when they find their way into our soil, water and air.

Sustainable development can bring about harmony, balance and justice between peoples, and between our human species and nature. It can come only with single-minded and unalterable devotion and effort.

No one of us on the global common is exempt from the dangers of environmental disaster. So no one of us can "be excused" from the exercise of our individual and mutual responsibilities.

The rules-of-survival are as immutable as the laws of physics. There will be no "pardons" for us if we fail to obey, and respond to the iron imperatives we now recognize and understand; there may not even be anyone to write our obituary.

Chapter Three

THE WORLD'S ECONOMY

Since the Fifties, vast improvements in communications and transportation mean the impact of industrial nation policies on developing world economies and environments is practically instantaneous. When any sector of the business, finance, and industrial community in the "West" catches cold, Third World nations begin to sneeze - and they have far fewer resources to combat the globe's economic ills. Mostly, in the period since World War Two, "First World" economic decisions have been against the interests, even the survival, of the Third World.

To ensure development we can live with, two pre-conditions are essential:

1. We must guarantee the survival of the ecosphere, everywhere on the planet.

2. "East-West" or "North-South" economic partners must both be satisfied of the justice of their mutual arrangements.

So far the world is largely divided into "those who do," and "those who are done-unto." What the industrial world has been "doing unto" the Third World scarcely bears scrutiny. The governments of industrial nations, along with their transnational banks and industries, seem still unaware of the dangers we all face when our neighbour's house is on fire. The danger to one's own home and security can only be exacerbated when one owns the mortgage on the neighbour's house! The wiser of our transnational agencies and corporations have been smelling the smoke for the past two decades. It's about time we organized an international bucket brigade.

Some efforts to rationalize international trade and finance in line with the needs for sustainable development have been made; but there's been little evidence of the sense of urgency needed to move as quickly and aggressively as we must.

Winston Churchill summed-up the need rather well, in a speech to Britain's Parliament in February, 1944:

"It is better to be frightened now than killed hereafter."

In 1946, speaking in the United States at a university in Fulton, Missouri, England's wartime leader made direct reference to the ungoverned dominance of technology and the possible consequences for mankind:

"The dark ages may return; the Stone Age may return on the gleaming wings of science . . . Time may be short."

Briefly put: the economic and trade policies of the industrial world have chiefly served to multiply and compound the problems, economic and environmental, of the developing world. We've already seen how increasing debt charges and falling commodity prices have forced Third World countries to abuse and over-exploit resources; they cut timber faster than it can be replaced, causing soil erosion and future flooding as well as wiping out a renewable resource base; the same too often applies, as we've seen, to farming and fishing.

Every increase in interest rates, every drop in commodity prices, every new tariff, and every screw tightened in the growing structure of Western protectionism adds to the momentum of the Third World's headlong spiral into poverty and environmental disaster.

An example:

Five nations in the Sahel region of Africa, (south of the Sahara Desert) - Burkino Faso, Chad, Mali, Niger and Senegal, increased their annual cotton production 6.78 times in the period between 1962 and 1983 (from twenty-seven million tonnes to 154 million tonnes). While production was rising during these two decades, world cotton prices fell steadily; so even vastly increased production failed to let these sub-Saharan nations keep up with escalating international debt. At the same time, the Sahel region set a less salubrious record:

In the early Sixties the Sahel region as a whole imported 200,000 tonnes of cereals annually. In 1984 the region had to import 1.77 million tonnes of cereals - almost nine times the figure of twenty years earlier. Some of the increase can be laid at the door of larger population; much more blame is clearly attributable to land taken out of food production to produce the cotton needed for export to pay debt charges. Even this equation fails to factor-in the probably massive destruction of arable land by over-cultivation of cotton crops.

The western world has, to its credit, moved effectively in emergency aid with regard to the drought in sub-Saharan Africa, the floods in Bangladesh, etc. But almost every industrial nation has failed to meet the foreign aid goals all have accepted: three-quarters of one percent of annual GNP. The consequence, for the Third World, is that net flows of resources - money and goods, have actually fallen in real terms in the past decade.

Moreover, the amount of capital expected to be sent to the Third World in the balance of this decade represents only half the amount needed to restore economic growth and stem the rising tide of poverty.

Larger volumes of resources from the rich nations to the poor, in loans and aid, in trade and technology, are vital to survival of the global village. Those resource exchanges must improve both in quantity and in quality - the targeting of processes and procedures to foster development we can live with.

The charge that new flows of capital to the Third World have moved into a deficit position is no woolly bit of theorizing. Consider:

-    In 1979, there was a "net transfer" to the Third world of $41.4 billion. (This including loans, aid, and investment, after allowing for Third World costs of interest payments, returns on investment to foreign developers, etc.) In 1985, these same countries, excluding Latin America, had a net DEFICIT of $31 billion. In Latin America, the area with the greatest burden of foreign debt, the numbers changed from a net inflow of $15.6 billion in 1979 to an outflow of $30 billion in 1985!

Overall, the developing nations are losing ground steadily; between 1980 and 1985, population growth outran economic growth in almost every developing state.

In their desperate efforts to survive, many Third World nations, most especially those in sub-Saharan Africa, have accepted austerity programmes dictated by the International

31

Monetary Fund: this as a prerequisite to receiving the credit they must have, just to meet international debt interest payments. As a direct result of these draconian measures, all these nations have had to severely cut social and environmental programmes. Austerity, it turns-out, is merely a new and painful form of slow-motion economic suicide: this because the burgeoning poverty created by austerity - the rising unemployment, hunger, urban crowding, et al merely pour more fuel on the flames of environmental destruction via over-use of resources and declining standards of health and education.

Sub-Saharan Africa and Latin America have become templates for planetary destruction. No better patterns could be found for human, economic and ecological self-immolation. Rather than proceed with mindless austerity programmes, the Western world could reach the same ends more efficiently, and with no greater pain, by defoliating and napalming Third World agricultural resources. The entire process of spiraling debt payments, plummeting commodity prices and Western protectionism adds up to a form of genocide-by-default.

It's been said, "truth is the first casualty of war." It would seem, in our war for the survival of the global village, rationality is the primary victim. **It's both ironic and self-destructive that conservation is generally ignored in times of economic hardship, when it's most needed.**

The current equations-of-destruction are numbingly simple:

a) Poverty and hunger lead to environmental destruction which leads to:

- More poverty and hunger.

b) Higher interest rates and lower commodity prices lead to lower savings and less investment which mean:

-      More poverty, fewer services, less employment and an explosion of poverty, hunger and all their economically disastrous consequences.

The vicious circle/cycle can be reversed.

Witness South Asia, where a Sixties crisis similar to today's situation in Africa and Latin America has been turned-around. In South Asia generally, population growth is down; savings, investment and employment are up; literacy rates, food production, even life expectancy, have begun to rise; environmental management and long-term technological development and planning are becoming the norm.

That is not happening in Africa and Latin America. Despite massive increases in production, cash income from trade had **dropped** ten percent in sub-Saharan Africa between 1970 and 1985. In the past decade, prices for cotton, sugar, timber, rubber, copper, iron ore, even ground nuts (peanuts) and cocoa have all fallen sharply.

In 1980, the sub-Saharan African states had to use fifteen percent of their export earnings to pay interest on foreign debt. By 1985 the proportion of earnings diverted to debt servicing had more than doubled, to thirty-one percent.

Hungry people, it must be remembered, are inefficient workers. They produce less, earn less, help their nation's recovery less.

The long-term aid now planned for Africa is not enough. Without dramatic change in the levels of aid, the problems will get worse.

International debt threatens the industrial world's stability as much as that of developing nations. This not least because folk who are deeply in debt stop being consumers. A case in point:

- Thirty percent of the globe's international debt (of roughly $950 billion) is owed by four Latin American nations: Mexico, Brazil, Venezuela and Argentina.

- Latin American imports from the industrial world have fallen by forty percent, in real terms, over the past three years.

There's no coincidence there - simply cause and effect.

One more figure for the litany of despair in Latin America: almost forty percent of Latin American export earnings now are used just to service international debt. That leaves very little hard currency to buy any products or services from the West.

Ask any investor, any international banker, any executive of a transnational industry their first priority when operating in a foreign state. All will give the same answer:

Stability. Now consider this:

Stability is the least likely prognosis in any country where social and educational services are being cut, unemployment increasing, urban crowding and dislocation exploding - and all because of rising foreign debt payments, slumping commodity prices and accelerating Western protectionism. That fact is crucial to the industrial world where, between 1960 and 1980, the share of mineral imports from the Third World (other than oil) used in manufacturing rose from nineteen to thirty percent. Yet commercial and international lending to the Third world has fallen sharply during the same period. The bankers have proved to be "fair weather friends" to developing nations. When times were good, the western banks were competing to loan money to the Third World; as global recession tightened the noose on growth, interest rates rocketed to historic levels and the tap was disconnected.

Simple survival dictates large increases in the money made available to the World Bank and the International Monetary fund - and increases in global lending by the commercial banks. But the "quality" of loans is a paramount consideration.

In the past, loans for fishing, farming, timber and industrial projects have focused on tunnel-visioned, short term profits rather than enduring, sustainable development. That's not good enough, anymore. Hit-and-run projects in the Third World are entirely analogous to the smash-and-grab thief who heaves a brick through a jewelry store window, and runs away with a handful of rings and watches. We've left too many broken windows in developing nations.

Broadly speaking, small-scale development holds the best hope for environmentally-sound growth. We need to "tie" less of our aid to Western commodities and materials and put a much larger proportion of aid into grass-roots programmes. Too many countries, like Canada, "tie" their aid by insisting money "given" to a developing country be spent on needlessly costly goods and services from the "donor" nation. That may be good domestic politics. It is lousy economics.

Happily, the World Bank has now decided to make environmental factors central to its loan decisions and project evaluations. This is crucial because other lending institutions - and governments, tend to use World Bank procedures and priorities as benchmarks for their own activities. The International Monetary Fund should follow the lead of the World Bank. Beyond this, the World Bank and IMF should develop methodologies for environmental impact studies and plans which can be "transferred" to Third World nations.

In trade terms, the developing nations cannot survive, let alone prosper, if the rising and self-defeating tide of Western protectionism defeats their efforts to diversify their economies.

As of now, in what are called the "least developed nations" - the poorest of the Third World countries - seventy-three percent of all exports are from sales of primary commodities. That figure is a recipe for economic disaster. In 1985, the United Nations Conference on Trade and Development estimated world commodity prices (excluding oil) had **dropped thirty percent since 1980** - in both real and dollar terms.

While the industrial world has begun to pull out of the recession of the early Eighties (only, perhaps, to face another in the Nineties), the developing nations have failed to improve their lot - commodity prices are still at their nadir - not least because, desperate to earn funds to pay foreign debt, the Third World nations have accelerated production and, thereby, created stockpiles and surpluses which have depressed prices even further. Nor do producers in developing nations have the shock-absorbing price supports, grants and tax breaks offered farmers, mineral producers and others in industrial nations. Some system of price stabilization is fundamental to Third World prosperity and growth.

Where non-renewable resources are concerned, Third World governments should insist:

a) Any leaseholder/exploiter should guarantee to undertake exploration sufficient to prove new reserves at least equal to those being removed.

b) The ratio of production to proven reserves must be kept at a fixed and sustainable level.

c)   Funds generated by royalties must be earmarked, to the appropriate degree, for development which can replace exhausted, non-renewable resources. (The so-called "Heritage Fund" instituted in Alberta, Canada, from petroleum royalty revenues provides an interesting case study in this area.)

d)   Resource exploiters must be held responsible for environmental control measures and restoration of land and other resources dislocated during extraction of resources. (A classic example of the failure of industry in this area can be seen in the barren, eroded hillsides and valleys of Appalachia following strip-mining in the American states of Kentucky, Virginia, Missouri et al; another can be seen [by air] on the west coast of British Columbia, in Canada, where "clear cutting" of timber has created irreversible erosion of denuded mountainsides.)

Most Third World nations lack the experience, the expertise, or the resources to police resource development efficiently. They need our help. The World Bank, the IMF, western aid agencies and UN agencies should - indeed, must - coordinate plans to make the necessary level of skills and resources available to our neighbours in the global village.

We are not helping much, at the moment. A case in point:

The industrial West has been promoting the production of sugar beets, to the detriment of sugar cane exporters. Let's see why that matters:

a) Sugar beet production is highly capital intensive.

b) Sugar beet production depends heavily on the use of chemical herbicides and, because of the way it leaches nutrients from the soil, has much less capacity to regenerate and produce in successive years than sugar cane.

c)   Thirty million Third World people depend, for their entire livelihoods, on sugar cane production. The national economies of many nations, including Fiji, Mauritius and several Caribbean islands (including Cuba) depend entirely on sugar cane exports.

d)   Sugar cane can be produced much more cheaply, is labour intensive, does far less ecological damage, and can preserve a number of Third World national economies. Yet the industrial world persists in promoting sugar beet production to woo agricultural voters.

There are "double standards" at work throughout the industrial world's relations with the Third World. They are just as destructive as the double standards traditional in sexist, western society. Example:

If industrial state transnationals had to meet the same pollution standards required of them "at home" in their activities in the Third World, their costs, in 1980 alone, would have risen by $14.2 billion! That, one must add, is a conservative estimate. Those numbers do not include the costs of environmental damage done by the transnationals in the developing nations.

Sadly, as industrial states export environmentally and occupationally dangerous technology no longer acceptable "at home," Third World politicians often see the transfer of destructive technologies and "pollution intensive" systems as an "opportunity" to develop industry and employment. So Indonesia and other nations have a whole new generation of "grannies" - young women whose sight has been afflicted by the fumes from solvents used to clean microchip components in radio, computer and tv assembly systems. Tobacco companies send their high tar products to the Third World with the rationale that "folk in the Third World like stronger cigarettes." Environmentally obsolete or downright dangerous technology, products, and processes frequently find their way to developing nations:

In Canada, when U.S. markets closed to asbestos products, the government invested millions to market that life-destroying product in the Third World, where there was, in the memorable words of a senior spokesman for the Mines Ministry, "less market resistance."

A typical Third World result of such self-serving, myopic policies: a ditch in Sri Lanka where one can, literally, see lethal asbestos fibres floating on the water emitted by an asbestos factory - a factory built with foreign aid. (One may, in such cases, be pardoned for regarding the word "aid" as a misnomer.)

The short answer: the transnationals of the industrial world must, like their governments, begin to play **a direct role** in fostering sustainable development. We have too many slow-motion Bhopals en route to disastrous fulfillment in the Third World.

The transnationals dominate the world in primary commodities trade. So the world's environmental development problems cannot be solved without their participation. Nor can the transnationals survive this century or the next without those solutions.

We've already observed the utter futility of assuming developing nations can resolve all of their own problems without outside help. They lack not only the resources but also the control. As an example:

Between eighty and ninety percent of all the world's trade in tea, coffee, cocoa, cotton, forest products, tobacco, jute, copper, iron ore, and bauxite is controlled, in each case, by a cartel of the three to six largest Western transnationals.

So it is not that the transnationals "will have" a role to play; they are major players now. What's needed is a change in the ground rules and a reassessment of the objects of the game. Most developing nations must bargain from weakness when dealing with the transnationals. Not only do these international giants control most commodities as noted above, the annual budget of most major transnationals is often greater than the entire GNP of Third World countries where they operate. Small wonder these often tiny and usually poor nation states take what they are offered by the world's corporate behemoths. What's on offer most often is exploitation of minerals, as we've seen, and the "export" of pollution-intensive industry to the Third World.

At present, as one instance, about one-quarter of all direct investment in the Third World by the United Kingdom, the United States and Japan is in the chemical industry - maybe the industry with the highest rate of environmental risk. Agriculture, mining and other extractive industries use up another twenty-five to thirty percent of major Western investment in the developing nations.

Until there is "a level playing field" between the industrial conglomerates and the Third World there can be neither equity, trust nor effectual plans for a safe environment.

It is both a critical and urgent task to strengthen the bargaining position of Third World nations in their dealings with transnationals. Regional and international institutions can and must help. **Technical assistance and advisory teams must be made available to work with individual countries when they go to the bargaining tables.** These squads of skilled advisors would function as roving global SWAT teams - protecting the environment and its chief dependents, the citizens of each nation. The resources brought to each negotiation by these environmental/developmental strike teams would include comprehensive data on the standards applied to environmentally hazardous processes and products in the home countries of the transnationals; this to help guarantee these same levels of environmental protection are exported to the Third World, along with investment and the other elements of exploitation.

There must also be an urgent and concerted effort to add the pragmatic realities of environment and sustainable development to rules-of-the-road for transnationals operating in the Third World. Both the OECD and the United Nations should take a lead in adding these critical issues to current discussion of international, corporate codes of behaviour.

A far greater exchange and transfer of technology is crucial to developing the kind of growth we can live with. An organized and deliberate effort to develop new technology is essential. Corporations and governments cannot, anymore, justify hoarding information.

To claim patent, copyright or vested-interest protection of crucial knowledge in today's shrinking world is an act of wanton, global negligence. It is as though, seeing someone bleeding to death on the roadside, we refused to explain how to tie a tourniquet.

In 1980 alone, developing countries paid the industrial West about $2 billion in royalties and fees for scientific and technological data and products. That system may make short-term economic sense to individual corporations, but given the thin resources of Third World nations, it makes mockery of efforts to sustain our global resources. Even in terms of Western survival, the system of charging developing nations for essential technological knowledge is about as sensible as charging our neighbours for cholera vaccine when we know their plague will surely infect our children, too, if we do not help them avoid the disease.

Proprietary rights spring from a system the world may no longer be able to afford. We all do share proprietary rights in global survival; we can only protect those rights through a system of international cooperation and control.

Infinitely more research is needed, though not necessarily infinitely more money. Most international research and development funds are now spent in pursuit of military goals; a smaller amount goes to enhance the commercial objectives of large corporations. One assumes the globe would survive without the investment of millions of dollars to research and develop an infantry rifle weighing four ounces less than the current model; the sum could better be spent developing new generations of productive cereal seed, economic village biogas systems, or safe water technology.

Biotechnology is an acutely vital area of development for Third World survival and success. Developing nations can do a lot through the establishment of cooperative, co-funded regional research centres. The industrial states must help.

The West must also assist developing nations in their expansion of export trade, especially in areas which will sustain rather than demolish resources. The economies of Third World states must be given the "kick start" needed to bring them to a level at which they will become self-propelling. This means reversing current trends:

Rising protectionism and declining international cooperation and multilateral agreement have been the depressing pattern of the past decade. Isolationism and navel-gazing preoccupation are no longer luxuries we can afford. Our global lifeboat is almost dead in the water; if we leave all the rowing to those folk on the other side of the vessel, we will continue to simply turn in circles of futility. We have adequate charts to survival, and sound compasses to locate the direction of sustainable growth; both are useless so long as we rest on our oars.

Chapter Four

POPULATION IN
THE GLOBAL VILLAGE

There are a series of ironic equations associated with population. Some examples:

a) Poverty breeds population. When a large proportion of infants and children die, big families are the only "pension plan" poor families can arrange.

b) Some aid-giving nations (most specifically, the U.S.) disapprove, politically, some methods of population control (most particularly state-supported abortion); so they refuse to support Third world population control schemes. The result is exploding populations which eat up far more aid funds in medical and food relief.

c) The finite resources of our global village cannot support an infinitely-growing population. But we do need more people to develop the resources we have - especially trained and skilled people.

That said, present rates of population growth cannot continue if we are all to survive. At the beginning of 1985 we were 4.8 billion people; eighty million more were added to our number in that year alone. By 1990 we were 5.29 billion and projections are that we will add another billion souls in this decade - more than ninety-six million annually. More critically, most population growth is in poor families and in regions where resources are already stretched to the breaking point. Another irony:

One person added to the population of the industrial world uses at least as much of the globe's resources as thirty-or-more Third World children.

Just as we must improve the quality of aid and development, so we must increase the quality of life for all the earth's people; they must have the resources to better realize their full potential; to improve individual, human productivity. At the same time, social support systems are essential to persuade poor families they need not depend on large families as their only source of income when they grow older.

The most effective means of family planning and population control is adult, female literacy.

Literate women marry later, space their children, and have smaller families. So no global effort to reduce population growth can be effectual without a major and calculated effort to foster women's rights. Self-determination for women is basic to the salvation of our global village. Education and the increment in self-determination which follows are dependent on development. So, the final irony, if you will:

We can only grow our way out of the population explosion. Without more development we cannot hope to curb the current, ungovernable increases in population.

Another point: regardless of current efforts, the world's population will continue to expand over the next thirty years, or more. The momentum already in place cannot be reversed in this generation.

It's said the quarter-mile long super oil tankers, if thrown into reverse, can't stop in in a distance of less than four miles; this because of their momentum through the water. Our population growth is like that. More specifically:

- In the developing nations, at least four people in every ten are under fifteen years of age. Contrast those figures with the industrial world where only two-in-ten are fifteen or younger. The consequences are simple:

The youthful population "bulge" in the Third World means populations will continue to grow over the next two or three generations; this as these children reach marrying and child-bearing age.

(By contrast, eleven percent of industrial state citizens are more than sixty-five years old compared to a mere four percent in developing nations; so, in the Western nations, more and more resources will go to the support of the elderly who already use a vastly disproportionate share of medical and social budgets.)

We must, in any event, begin with the realization there is no "magic bullet," no immediate panacea, for population growth. Family sizes are being reduced and population stabilized in much of the world, most notably in Asia; but in the global context we are going to grow a lot more before we stabilize, no matter how intense and effectual our efforts.

The obvious question: Can we feed that growing number of inhabitants in our global village? The answer is a conditional "yes":

A joint study by the Food and Agriculture Organization (FAO) and the International Institute for Applied Systems Analysis indicates we can feed one-and-one-half-times our projected population in the year 2000, (6.1 billion people); this even with a low level of agricultural technology. The survey covered 117 nations and provides figures for aggregate food production. The situation is less hopeful in many individual nations - where sixty-four countries with a total population of 1.1 billion cannot now feed themselves. Even with advanced agricultural technology there would be nineteen countries unable to produce sufficient food for themselves; however, these countries, mostly small island states, have generally higher incomes than the worst-off, and can afford to import foodstuffs.

The "theoretical" potential for global food production is stunning: Given the best appropriate technology, it's estimated the roughly 1.5 billion hectares now under cultivation could yield two-and-a-half times as much food as at present (up from an average of two tonnes of grain - or its equivalent - to five tonnes per hectare, per year.)

Note: There's a roughly equal amount of additional arable land, now used as permanent pasture, much of which could be cultivated.

Ignoring that vast bank of pasture, add the production from rangelands and from marine resources and the annual total of food production is believed capable of reaching eight billion tonnes of grain equivalent annually - enough to feed eleven billion people at current consumption levels. However, these levels, in the Third World, are grossly inadequate; if nutrition levels rise to a reasonable and healthy level, the world's "carrying capacity" with regard to the food/population equation is nearer 7.5 billion.

As we've noted, economic development reduces fertility rates. So international policies which impede Third World development - include Western protectionism and low commodities prices among those - have a literal and direct effect, a counterproductive effect, on population planning in our developing nations.

Conversely, almost any activity to increase material comfort, well-being and human security reduces the tendency to have more children than individual families (and the nations where they live) can comfortably sustain.

Population explosions are no new phenomenon. They began, in the mid-seventeen hundreds, with the Industrial Revolution in Europe, and the parallel improvement in farming techniques. Our more recent and urgent problems date back only to about 1950. In the industrial world of Europe, Japan and North America, population multiplied by a factor of five between 1750 and 1950. But the industrial West had a safety valve: between 1880 and 1910 alone, twenty percent of the population increase was siphoned-off by emigration. No similar solution is available to the Third World today.

Current estimates say the world will have a population of 8.2 billion by 2025. Some developing nations (Cuba, Sri Lanka and China as examples) already have well-stabilized population growth rates.

-    If population stabilizes by 2010 (a difficult goal) the globe will "level-off" at about 7.76 billion people by 2060.

-    If stabilization isn't reached until 2035, the total world population will settle at 10.2 billion in 2095 - a total very near the maximum food-carrying capacity of the global village, as noted earlier.

-    If we fail to halt our population explosion until 2065, seventy-five years from now, we'll have a population by 2100 of 14.2 billion. Since, at best estimates, we can feed only eleven billion, one has to assume mass starvation, in the order of as many people as are now alive on earth, in such a "worst case scenario."

Demography plays as great a role in population equations as birth rates: since 1950, for example, the total number of city dwellers has quadrupled in the developing nations. The subsequent social, economic and political pressures have been horrendous; they will multiply as these cities continue to grow.

(Example: In Colombo, the capital city of Sri Lanka, the antiquated water and sewerage system installed by the British colonial regime almost one hundred years ago was meant to serve a population one-tenth the size of today's. No Third World government has the means to refurbish, modernize and expand such systems to meet today's needs, let alone those of next year - or the next century.)

It's interesting to note life expectancy has risen and infant mortality rates have fallen almost everywhere in the world. Interesting, too, to observe similar changes were experienced in the industrial West **before** the advent of modern antibiotics and other "miracle drugs." In the West, fifty years ago, as in the Third World today, the major change followed improved education, nutrition and hygiene. A further point, lest those in the "West" become arrogant about their progress:

Life expectancy was lower, and infant mortality rates higher, in New York, Tokyo, Berlin, Paris, Rome and London, in 1920, than is now the case in Bangladesh, Haiti, Ethiopia, Brazil. The Third World is, in terms of 10,000 years of recorded human history, just a hiccup behind the industrial world. Nor is poverty alone the barrier.

In some areas, India's southwest Kerela state and Sri Lanka are notable examples, high literacy rates have resulted in low fertility figures, low infant mortality and high life expectancy despite average incomes much lower than in surrounding areas. These successes must be duplicated throughout the developing world if we are to manage our global village for everyone's benefit - and everyone's survival. For a start, politicians and other policy-makers must understand "productive" or "economic" policies are indivisible from social policies:

Increasing human potential towards its ultimate capacity is our greatest task. That can be accomplished only with reduced family size in the Third World, and the freedom and power-of-choice that change will bring to women and, thereby, their families.

At this time, only fifteen cents of every ten dollars spent on foreign aid goes to help in population programmes. That's not enough. Moreover family planning and child-spacing programmes are usually isolated from other development goals. The most successful schemes have combined family planning with literacy programmes, rural development, water and sanitation projects:

In Zimbabwe, early efforts to help women "space" their children have led, unexpectedly, to greatly reduced family size. Zimbabwe now leads all sub-Saharan Africa - still the area of highest fertility in the world - in reduced birth rates.

When more children die, parents choose to have larger families. It matters then that 1.7 billion people, more than enough to populate every major city on the globe, still lack access to safe water supplies. Almost as many, 1.2 billion, have no functional sanitation facilities.

To assess the potential for a healthy existence in any developing country, don't count the number of available hospital beds: count the safe village wells and water taps, the latrines - and the schoolrooms.

Industrial and growth policies must, in future, be governed and assessed on the basis of their impact on public health, environment, occupational safety, and effect on human settlements. No other criteria are sufficient.

The World Health Organization's "Health For All" strategy must be broadened beyond concern for medical workers and clinics: only holistic measures can save the global village. "Health For All" is a chimera, an illusion, until we make concerns-for-health central to every developmental activity.

Current efforts to make immunization, and oral rehydration therapy for diarrhea victims universally available are fundamental to our mutual self-respect, and our survival. One child dies every six seconds, in the Third World, from the dehydration caused by diarrhea. (That's five million deaths, every year - as many kids dead, every six years, as everyone killed in World War Two.) *Yet most deaths from diarrhea - deaths caused by dehydration - can be prevented by mothers trained to make and administer "oral rehydration fluid", a simple mixture of water (even polluted water) with sugar and salt. This "miracle cure" costs less than five cents to prepare; the poorest Third World mothers have the necessary ingredients.* Another child perishes every six seconds for lack of immunization. Last year, measles killed two million kids - a number equal to the entire population of Montreal or Toronto.

As life styles change in developing nations, new threats to health arise. Two hundred years ago, Europe "exported" syphilis, typhoid, smallpox and tuberculosis to the New World. Today's exportable illnesses will include cancer and heart disease, especially so long as industrial nations ship their highest-tar tobaccos to developing nations. So better public health education is now mandatory in the Third World.

We must, too, stop being hesitant about Acquired Immune Deficiency Syndrome. AIDS is now a fact-of-international-life. Millions are going to die of AIDS; in parts of the Third World, whole societies and economies may be disrupted. Another case of "our neighbours's house on fire." It's time we smelled the smoke, and summoned the fire brigade; our home, too, is threatened.

Many powerful resources to aid in our mutual survival are being ignored, or under-exploited. Examples:

- In Egypt and other Muslim states, UNICEF uses Koranic verses to emphasize the lessons of sanitation, child health protection, immunization, et al. The "imams," or religious leaders, read the verses in the mosques. Religious organizations around the world represent an enormous tool for development, health and survival.

- So, too, do such groups as boy scouts and girl guides: already, twenty-five million of these youngsters have been enlisted to help implement global immunization programmes.

But we are falling behind. The gaps between rich and poor are spreading. Illiteracy is rising despite major efforts to improve educational access in the Third World. By the year 2000 there will be 900 million of our global neighbours who can neither read nor write. That is one person in every four living today, unable to write their name on a voters' list, lacking the knowledge to avoid being cheated at the village market without the basic skills of reading and arithmetic, unequipped to make life and death decisions for themselves or their children about health care, immunization, nutrition, occupation.

In some Ethiopian nursery schools, four- and five-year-old children must each plant a tree on their first day in class - and water and cultivate their seedling daily. Such lessons in conservation, aforestation and survival are essential to reclaiming, restoring and retaining our global village. They should, indeed they must be copied around the world.

We still fail miserably in public education. Architects regularly dedicate one percent of the total cost of an office tower to "aesthetics" - fountains, sculpture, ceramics and murals; but most foreign aid funds fail to allocate a sou/nickel/farthing/yen to public education. Radio and television probably offer the best teaching tool since the original log, with an instructor on one end and pupil on the other; we've utterly failed to use these best-of-all-possible means of changing attitudes and upgrading skills.

Finally, in examining the globe's population, it's time we devoted some special attention to those small pockets of tribal and "indigenous" peoples who have been the chief victims of much recent development. Many such groups live in isolation; many have suffered virtual cultural extinction at the hands of "developers" in Latin America and elsewhere. We owe these global village neighbours choices:

We must not either keep them in artificial and unwanted isolation, nor destroy their life-styles and cultures through mindless development. Nature has countless examples for us of the strengths of diversity. We can no more afford to sacrifice any human culture than any strain of plants, any animal, fish or bird species.

Fifty years ago, Winston Churchill told the Parliament at Westminster,

"No man is free, while any man is unjustly imprisoned."

So, today:

"No man or woman is safe, in our global village, when their neighbour is threatened."

Chapter Five

FEEDING THE GLOBAL VILLAGE

Despite population increase, we now produce more food per capita than ever before in human history. Cereals and root crops are still the primary source of food, globally; in 1985 we grew nearly five hundred kilos of them for everyone then alive in the world. Of course all the cereal and tuber foods produced weren't "for" all of us after all; in the same year there were 730 million of us without enough food even to function normally and productively. About three times the entire population of the United States, that is, goes hungry every year - so hungry they lack the physical and mental stamina to work or study effectively. The causes of food shortages clearly vary with regions:

- In some places too little food is grown.
- In some areas there's enough food, but families haven't the money to buy it.
- In other regions, the greatest threat to future food supply is over-production today and consequent soil damage in future.

We have the skills, the knowledge and technology to feed everyone. We don't have policies to see food produced and distributed according to human need. Nor have we fully acknowledged the slow motion disasters created by chronic malnutrition. Starvation, it's true, kills. But chronic malnourishment is the assassin of hope; it saps the will to achieve, cripples and wastes both mind and body, leaves its victims easy prey to both physical and social ills.

World food trade has changed dramatically in the past thirty-five years. Cereal production increased two-and-one-half times in that period - and North American foodgrain exports twenty-four times (from five million tonnes to 120 million.) Meat production more than tripled in Europe in the

49

same period, and global meat exports rose five-and-one half-times, from two million tonnes to over eleven million. Pound-for-pound, the four billion cattle, sheep and pigs in our global village now outweigh the human population. But we now know we are losing fourteen million tonnes of grain production alone, every year, to soil erosion, air pollution and acid rain. As a direct result, food production increases are falling behind population increases by thirteen million tonnes per year.

Increased production since World War Two owes much to changing technology: twice as much land is irrigated as in 1950; but we are using nine times more chemical fertilizer and thirty-two times more pesticides. The result? We are also polluting the ground water over much of the planet. Nor have the production increases been uniform. For example, we are producing about fifteen million more tonnes of grain each year - but the figure needs to be 28 million tonnes.

In Africa, foodgrain production relative to Europe's has dropped by as much as twenty percent in some nations to an alarming fifty percent in others.

While large scale "agro-industry" has developed in the industrial states and the "green revolution" has taken hold in the lush heartlands of many developing nations, in most of sub-Saharan Africa and the remote areas of Asia and Latin America subsistence farming is still the rule, and hunger the norm. Moreover progress is slowing. After the surge of the Fifties and Sixties, the necessary three percent annual growth in food output was extremely difficult to sustain in the Eighties.

Africa has been experiencing an average one percent drop in per capita food production since the start of the Seventies. In Latin America, food production has kept pace with population growth; but the degradation of agricultural land, fueled largely by the foreign debt crisis, presages serious future difficulties.

Farm subsidies and surplus food supplies in the industrial states are posing critical problems for the Third World:

In the United States alone, farm subsidies rose about nine times (from $2.7 billion to $25.8 billion) in the five years between 1980 and 1986. There was a corresponding increase of almost four-and-a-half times in the European Economic Community in the decade following 1976 - from $6.2 billion U.S. to $26 billion. In Japan, rice prices are kept at an artificial level five times the world average; Japanese farmers are "protected" by laws making it a criminal offense to import even a few kilos of rice. Japan spends $10.5 billion in annual farm subsidies. Canada spends $3.4 billion. Worldwide, we spend more than $150 billion on these subsidies every year.

In many countries, Japan and Canada included, farm subsidies cost every man, woman and child from $100 to $150 dollars a year. That's an amount equal to from one-quarter to one-half of the entire per capita gross national product of many less developed nations. In many of these Third World nations, GNP is so low in part because local farmers are being undercut by subsidized, western world produce, be it grain, butter or sugar beets. In this context alone, industrial world farm subsidies are being paid, in an entirely real if indirect sense, by picking the pockets of Third World farmers and their children.

Heavily-subsidized food exports from Europe and North America depress world prices; and, by forcing down the income of subsistence Third World farmers, they destroy any incentive to increase domestic food production in developing nations. At the same time "protected" and subsidized food production in the industrial world has contributed to soil degradation, nitrate pollution of ground water through over-fertilization, and the destruction of marginal farmlands through clearing and over-cultivation.

The disruption of world markets by Western, subsidized agriculture must be eliminated.

In this context, the U.S. initiative announced in July, 1987, is more than welcome. The United states told a Geneva meeting of GATT (The General Agreement on Tariffs and Trade) it wanted to end the global agricultural war. (A war, one might add, in which the industrial states are using the equivalent of economic atom-bombs again Third World bows and arrows.) The U.S. proposed, over the next ten years, the world should:

Abolish *all* direct agricultural subsidies.

Abolish *all* indirect subsidies.

Abolish *all* protective barriers such as import quotas and tariffs.

Abolish *all* phoney indirect barriers such as health regulations by adopting international standards. (Canada, in the late Eighties, stopped "outside" competition with its domestic pork producers from low-cost imports of Danish bacon and ham effectually by nonsensically declaring thirty-two of thirty-four packing plants in Denmark were "unhygienic.")

Some observers and critics call the U.S. proposals "unrealistic," "unachievable," even "pipe dreams." They are, in blunt fact, essential.

Small farmers in the Third World, particularly in Asia, have shown a marked ability to use modern technology, when they are shown how. But small, cash crop farmers haven't the cash to invest in expensive equipment for their individual farms of one or two hectares. Even the purchase of a small, two-wheeled hand tractor is far beyond their means. The encouragement and stimulation of cooperative ventures maybe represents the best hope for more efficient and economic use of these smallholder farm plots.

At present, global agricultural policy seems predicated on the principle of short-term gain with the built-in certainty of long-term pain. We have soil erosion in North America (in Canada alone, erosion steals one billion dollars annually from farmers.) In Europe the cardinal problem is soil acidification. Asia, Africa and Latin America suffer from both desertification and deforestation.

Industrial policies, too, can steal precious farmland from our children - and their children. Before our grandchildren are old enough to bear children of their own, global warming caused by energy use and industrial production may cause flooding of vital, coastal farm lands.

By the late Seventies, soil erosion exceeded soil formation on one-third of U.S. cropland, and affected thirty percent of all farmland in India. According to an FAO (UN Food and Agriculture Organization) study, we are eventually going to lose 544 million hectares of rain-fed cropland. More graphically, this means one-third of the world's farms destroyed - an area of 1.87 million square miles - **that's equal to the combined land areas of France, Germany, India, Italy and Spain!**

Soil erosion does more than denude farms. The topsoil washed-away silts-up ports and water reservoirs, increases flooding, and ultimately presents an extortionate bill to aid-giving nations.

Even irrigation, when not carefully planned, brings hazards: these include salinization, alkalization and the waterlogging of soil. These problems are now causing farmers to abandon 10 million hectares of irrigated land every year - **as much as the land area of Hungary, the whole of Austria or the entire U.S. State of Maine.**

The overuse of chemicals in agriculture destroys more than land, though that damage eventually results in hunger and human death. More directly, 10,000 people in the Third World are being killed by pesticide poisoning alone every year. Almost a half-million individuals every year - roughly equal to the total population of Cleveland or of Oslo - are severely injured, often permanently. Again, the industrial world bears a heavy responsibility. Some brief cases in point:

a) "Phosvel," a very effective insecticide, was banned from production and sale in the U.S. a decade ago; this after factory workers were shown to have suffered irreversible nerve damage while manufacturing the stuff. The insecticide is still being marketed, by the U.S. firms, in Central America.

b) Another pesticide, DBCP (dibromochlopropane) cannot be made or sold in the U.S., as it destroys human sperm and renders men sterile. After it was banned, almost a decade ago, millions of pounds were shipped to Costa Rica for use as a "wormicide" on banana plantations. An estimated 2,000 Costa Rican plantation workers are now sterile; countless others have drastically-reduced sperm counts. *Documented medical evidence shows the American manufacturers, Dow Chemical and the Shell Company, knew the health hazards of DBCP twenty years before the product was banned in the United States and twenty-five years before the damage was done in Costa Rica.*

c) Among children in Costa Rica, cancer rates among

farm children under seven years have doubled in just ten years. Pesticide use has also doubled, in the same period. Costa Rica now has the highest rate of child leukemia in the world. The leukemia rate has doubled in twenty years.

Every year we lose, permanently, six million hectares of land to desertification. Call that 20,000 square miles - one-third more than the entire area of Switzerland or The Netherlands - every year.

Against these grim statistics is the naked necessity:

Until population is stabilized, we must increase global food production from three to four percent, every year, to stay alive. For starters, we can look to large areas of Latin America, North America, the Soviet Union and sub-Saharan Africa where unused lands could be brought into production. Caution and careful study will be essential, however, as the quality of these untapped areas varies greatly, and some are ecologically vulnerable.

We cannot solve the world's food problems by exporting food to the Third World. Developing nations which import food are effectually importing unemployment as farmers are forced off the land.

We've three key tasks:

1. Shifting production to the areas of greatest need.
2. Ensuring a decent living for the globe's poor.
3. Conserving resources.

Government farm policies worldwide must be examined and re-drafted so they will:

a) Include the environmental criteria which now mostly suffer at the hands of short term planning.

b) Develop the flexibility to assist with local and regional needs, rather than strapping all farm policies to a rigid national plan likely to be unsuitable for almost any area of special topography, climate, soil.

c) Stop over-protecting large-scale farmers and stimulating the forms of over-production which, in the long run, can only harm the global agricultural industry.

Price supports and controls generally benefit urban dwellers more than farmers; and they distort crop production patterns while adding to destructive pressure on our shrinking base of farmland.

Agricultural trade has increased six times since 1950. But there is still no rational pattern to our trade policies, if we are to leave our children a fertile planetary garden:

We need to identify global stress points, where land is endangered; and we must protect them as we now do cultural and historic sites.

We must begin to reclaim lands lost to acidification, deforestation and the rest. (In this regard, the current UN "Plan of Action To Combat Desertification" urgently needs more cash support.)

We must identify areas which, while not suitable for intense cultivation, can be used for fruit orchards, grazing land or forestry.

We have to encourage more use of organic plant nutrients, more emphasis on natural methods of pest control, more use of biogas or wind-generated pumps for irrigation. The industrial states must clamp down on controls related to the export of agricultural chemicals - especially pesticides.

Local, rural families in the developing nations are both the victims and the agents of deforestation, soil erosion, desertification. They must be directly and personally involved in reclamation and preventive measures.

"Agroforestry" techniques can produce both food, and fuel or timber, on the same land. Well-chosen crops reinforce one another in this system. The method is centuries-old in Asia where, today, pineapple is often planted between rubber or cocoa-nut palm trees in a system called "intercropping."

Fish farming is essential to developing enough protein for global consumption. Already one-tenth of all fisheries production, planet-wide, is from "aquaculture," or fish farming. By the year 2000 aquaculture production could equal the 100 million tonnes of fish we will be taking annually from our seas, rivers and lakes.

Most technical advances in agriculture in recent decades have been best-suited to fertile, stable soil conditions with good water supplies. Major research is needed to develop systems appropriate to the vast land masses with uncertain rainfall, uneven topography and less nourished soils. There will have to be major increases in funds available for agricultural research and extension work. These activities use up about 1.5 percent of gross farm income in prosperous nations, but only 0.9 percent in the developing world, where farm prices are also depressed.

As we noted in the last chapter, proprietary interests may also have to be re-thought. As of now, fifty-five percent of the world's plant genetic resources are controlled by institutions in industrial nations, though many originated in the Third World. All else aside, these developing nations may soon decide to stop sharing their genetic resources with Western organizations intent on sequestering the knowledge, and profiteering on the proceeds of that information.

Land reform, too, is an inescapable necessity. Any schemes must be worked-out nation-by-nation and region-by-region, as their circumstances vary widely and wildly. In every case, however, there must be a reform of tenancy arrangements, guaranteed security of tenure, and a clear recording of land rights. This matter is directly related to our need to make full use of our human resources. In terms of food production, one might accurately say female resources:

In Africa, for example, women do:
- Thirty percent of the plowing,
- Fifty percent of the planting,
- Seventy percent of the hoeing and weeding,
- Sixty percent of the harvesting,
- Eighty percent of the storing of food crops,
- Ninety percent of the processing,
- Sixty percent of the marketing of the produce.

Yet, in many nations, women cannot have title to farmland. In most, women are ignored at all levels of farm training and agricultural extension services. That situation **must** be reversed, if we are to feed ourselves and our children.

Finally, developing countries must be assisted in building "food banks" in surplus years to provide reserves against drought and crop failure. Emergency food relief from the industrial world is a frail reed.

The globe now has a reserve supply of only about one-fifth of average, annual need; two-thirds of that is in the industrial west - and half the balance is in India and China.

When food runs short in the Third World, income stops at the same time; so farmers can't buy what food is available. Food security, therefore, must include systems to give disaster-struck families cash to buy food.

(UNICEF tried this system, called "cash for food" in small parts of Ethiopia during the drought and famine of the mid-Eighties. The result: whole communities which would otherwise have been uprooted and moved to refugee feeding camps stayed on their land, dug irrigation canals and reservoirs and, when the rains returned, became self-sustaining, contributing members of their society.)

We can feed ourselves, and our children. We needn't take the food from the mouths of our children and grandchildren, as present practices threaten to do.

We must acknowledge, though, the fact most of our current agricultural policies were designed for a much more narrow, fragmented world. That world is gone. Our new realities demand we focus future policies on people, not technology - on resources, not production for its own, short term sake - on the long view, not the immediate gratification.

We are, surely, wise enough to avoid the folly of the grasshopper which, in the fable, failed to store food for the winter as he was too busy dancing; better the example of his friend the ant, who recognized the iron reality of future need and survived the time between harvests.

Better we plan now, and dance later, when we've more to celebrate.

Chapter Six

PROTECTING OTHER SPECIES
IN OUR WORLD

We don't know how many plant and animal species share our global village. We assume "a few million" survivors of the half-billion species which have existed since the earth was formed. Most, at a rate of one species every thirteen or fourteen months, have been destroyed by nature. Witness the dinosaur, the dodo, the hairy mammoth, even early ancestors in the family of man.

We also know humans now wipe-out entire species at a rate hundreds-of-times more rapid than nature's cruelest depredations. Nature, as we've just observed, has destroyed maybe one species every four hundred days. Humans are now killing off three species **every** day - call that 1200 species lost every four hundred days. In a decade the destruction could rise to three species per hour, or 26,000 species every year! And, we know some of the consequences:

Mostly we look to the scientific, esthetic and ethical consequences of eliminating a whole population of whooping cranes, orchids, or a sub-species of whales. We forget the far more wide-spread economic impact of lost species. Some examples:

a)   Organisms living on our coral reefs survive predators largely through undersea "chemical warfare." Science has used hundreds of these creatures to develop indispensable medical antidotes and treatments.

b)   In total, up to half of all prescription drugs are based on "wild" organisms. Worldwide, the annual commercial value of medication we would not have without "wild" or naturally indigenous species, is more than $40 billion. The figure will multiply as we learn and adapt more of nature's secrets through genetic engineering - and if those secrets aren't destroyed, with their species, before we learn them.

c)   In the United States alone, in 1980, the use of native, genetic plant materials (especially wild species of wheat and maize) contributed more than one billion dollars, every year, to farm income. The total is growing.

d)   In 1970, the U.S. lost $2 billion in maize crops to a leaf fungus. Fungus-resistant, wild strains of maize found in Mexico mean the problem will not recur.

e)   The most "primitive" sub-species of maize was found in Mexico more recently. Three tiny, wild plots totaling less than four hectares were about to be destroyed by farmers and loggers. The few thousand stalks found are now being cross-bred with commercial maize. Why?

This wild maize is the only known perennial species of maize. When the cross-breeding is successful, maize farmers, whether in Nigeria or Nebraska, will no more have to plow and seed their crops every year. The potential savings - call them increased profits - amount to many billions of dollars annually.

f)   Wildlife-derived products for modern industry include compounds almost beyond count. Start with waxes, resins, dyes, oils, vegetable fats, tannins, fibres and seeds far more oil-rich than any commercial plants. (In western Amazonia, the "Fevillea" genus of rain forest vine produces more oil per hectare, without cultivation, than a hectare of commercial oil palm plantation.)

g)   Plant species containing hydrocarbons (instead of the school-science-lesson truism of "plants being made-up of carbohydrates"), can flourish in areas laid waste, for example, by strip mining of coal. Imagine rehabilitating vast tracts with an annually renewable "petroleum plantation.'" With genetic engineering, we may soon discover elements in our world gene bank to produce food, even timber, in our deserts and in salt-corroded lands.

Even were we sufficiently short-sighted to assume we've all the plant diversity we need, we'd be foreclosing huge chunks of our future comfort, welfare and economy if we abandoned protection of "wild" species. Consider:

a)   The world's major cocoa-growing regions of West Africa would be out of business in a generation or so without the new genetic material from the forests of west Amazonia on which they are utterly dependent. You'd have no chocolate bars for your grandchildren.

b)   Columbian and Brazilian coffee crops would wither and disappear without regular injections of strains of wild coffee plants - mostly from Ethiopia.

c)   Southeast Asia's huge rubber production would skid to a halt without wild rubber germplasm from Brazil.

d)   Brazil's sugar cane and soybean production would soon dwindle away without similar transfers of plant germplasm from Asia.

Just as the basic root systems and stalks of the rose bushes in your garden, or your neighbour's, will fail to produce the flowers you want without grafting - from rose species you could not grow yourself - so with many of our most vital global crops.

The Seventies' oil crisis taught us the meaning of interdependence. We are even more crucially reliant on one another for diversity-of-species.

It's said we reproduce all the cells in our bodies, excepting nerve tissue, every seven years, as old tissue ages and dies. (We grow new skin cells even faster; witness the scrape on a child's arm.) We need proper fuel, healthy supplies of tissue-building brick and mortar to do that. Even so, our "genetic clocks" eventually refuse to go on renewing our vital parts. Those parts wear out, and our lives end. So with plants.

But we can do with them, the rubber and tea, the cocoa, coffee and soybeans, what we can't yet do for ourselves:

Given enough germplasm from "wild" or natural sources, we can keep them productive indefinitely. (In Sri Lanka one can find tea plants more than one hundred years old.) Hardly an option, surely, we want to abandon?

There is one chief difficulty in ensuring species/genetic preservation. (Without it, European and North America crops, too, would fade away as surely as coffee, rubber, cocoa.) The problem is rooted in our failure to recognize the pragmatic, economic imperatives and potentials. Most bluntly put, species protection is seen as a virtue rather than a need. We think of the "virtue" of protecting plant and animal species in patronizing terms, as a responsibility of the "superior" beings we assume ourselves to be. So far, we've not been "superior" enough to see, in the loss the these species, the same elements of our own destruction. Species protection, that is, is not seductive as a political issue. So its supporters so far lack political clout. The issue is well-down on the agenda-of-concern of industrialists, politicians, economists, even journalists. All pride themselves on being "realists" while in this case, ignoring one of the most fundamental realities of global survival. We seem, in this situation, more nearly related to the dinosaur, or the ostrich, than to even Cro-Magnon Man.

As is often the case, the public leads public leaders in this concern:

- More than 100,000 school children now belong to Kenya's Wildlife Clubs.

- The Audubon Society has over 385,000 members in the U.S. alone.

- Nature clubs in the Soviet Union comprise over 35 million members. With the break-neck social changes in view since the end of the Eighties, the USSR has even stopped planned construction of nuclear power plants in response to the voices of these activists.

There are scores of other examples around the globe.

The salient point is clear: we have, now, a global constituency-of-concern for species preservation. It remains to harness the public will **and use it as a generator for political will.** We've enough knowledge to make a valuable, indeed an essential, beginning. The problem now is not technological; it is political. So what needs doing, politically?

- First we must understand the integral links between the survival of our bank of plant and animal species and of global development.

- Second, we must begin to act on that conviction, both nationally and in relations and arrangements between countries.

We need to do far more research. *We've seriously studied only one percent of the world's plants - and even fewer of our animal species.* We can't even dream what medical, industrial, agricultural riches are being denied us by our self-imposed ignorance. Nor are we aware of the binding inter-relationships between plant and animal species. We do know a single insect or plant may sometimes be the keystone to a whole ecological structure. Yet we continue to casually lay waste to thousands of species before we've even understood the potential consequences, let alone given those consequences the consideration our survival demands.

We know, too, nature's life processes can be damaged or slowed only if we are willing to abandon the preservation of breeding grounds for our animal and fish life, the stabilization of our climate, the protection of our soil and our watersheds, the maintenance of those vast "nurseries" of timber and jungle.

The rain forests of the global village, along with timber stands worldwide and ocean algae, are the lungs of the world. We can't turn carbon dioxide back into oxygen; they do. To destroy our forests for short-term profit is as sensible as setting fire to our home to toast marshmallows.

Our descendants won't even know which blessings we've stolen from them: The species we are now busily destroying with deforestation, slash-and-burn farming, and the erosion of marginal lands, are precisely those about which we know least.

We should, instead, be developing a "Gene Revolution."

Governments and international agencies must select those species and strains most vital, most valuable, to our developmental needs. We must share and exchange both the knowledge and the benefits of that knowledge.

Most of our valuable genetic resources are in the tropics - that means in the developing nations. It's no longer sufficient to make withdrawals from this resource bank for the vastly disproportionate profit of the industrial states.

The expansion of livestock herding (still the most costly way of producing protein in terms of land, feed, and other resources used), threatens many species of plants. In arid and semi-arid lands, by way of example, plants which have adapted to local climate are amazingly hardy. Many have an extraordinary potential in the biochemical industry. Yet we may lose the chance to exploit the liquid wax of the "jojoba" shrub, the natural rubber of the "guayule" bush, and lose it to wandering herds of barrel-stave-ribbed cattle and the soil erosion attendant on the expansion of those nomadic herds.

We are, this and every year, totally eliminating an acreage of tropical rain forest equal to the area of Portugal - or double that of Denmark. By the century's end there may be almost no rain forest left outside the Zaire Basin of Africa and the western half of Brazilian Amazonia. Even these forests are unlikely to last the first few decades of the next century, given current policies of exploitation. This doesn't just entail the loss of forests, and of the planet's "lungs." It means, too, the absolute and permanent loss of up to seven of every ten plant, bird, and animal species in these areas - and the rain forests alone contain, exclusively, half the world's species.

Yet we began with 1.6 billion hectares of rain forest. We had, that is, 5.5 million square miles of rain forest on earth - almost double the entire area of Europe.

Our forests help stabilize our climate. Along with the seas, they act as a global thermostat. To lose them, as we are doing, will only hasten the "greenhouse effect" and dangerous "warming" of the climate over the next thirty years.

All our resources, and our uses of them, are closely interrelated. Damage one resource, weaken one brick or timber in our ecological home, and we endanger the entire structure. At present, to extend the analogy, we are taking developmental sledge hammers to whole walls; and we have no blueprints because we've not done the research.

One day soon we may, in our ignorance, destroy a main beam, and bring the whole, interdependent system down about our heads. More probably, we'll bury our children in the environmental rubble.

Government policies now frequently stimulate, almost demand, environmental and species destruction. Example:

Timber harvesting rights, especially in countries with rain forests, are usually short term. So concessionaires, to make a profit, move in quickly, without ecological studies. They take only the best trees, destroying maybe hundreds of young trees while "harvesting" each one they want. Nor are royalties, rents and taxes charged by governments hardly ever sufficient to reforest, and repair the damage.

Third World nations are the Aladdin's Cave of our plant and animal treasures, with over two-thirds of all of them within their borders. Medical researchers now believe this enormous "gene pool" will trigger more innovative, life-saving advances in the next twenty years than in the past two hundred. Those benefits also must be shared with the Third World - including the proprietary and employment and commercial gains.

Around the world, we must begin by developing National Conservation Strategies. These can be linked regionally and need not impose on national sovereignty. But we need a global "Species Convention" or treaty with the same international scope and outlook as, say, The Law Of The Sea Treaty. The International Union for the Conservation of Nature and Natural Resources (IUCN) has prepared such a treaty in draft form.

Any such agreement implies funding. As one possibility, each nation could contribute to a "species trust fund":

The chief beneficiaries of our global village resources would contribute proportionately. Payments to developing nations could rise and fall as those countries gave pragmatic demonstration of their ability to manage and preserve their resources.

Nationally, where park and nature preserve lands are a key element in preservation, they should more accurately be called "Development Parks," to stress their value as the genetic banks without which future growth is a dead letter.

International agencies - major lenders, including the World Bank as well as UN organizations - must give thorough and deliberate attention, regularly and systematically, to both the problems and opportunities of species conservation.

There is now a "Conservation Monitoring Centre" collating data on global species and ecosystems. This centre makes its data available worldwide. IUCN, working closely with the World Bank, the United Nations Environment Programme, and the World Wildlife Fund, should be expanded.

We have national "protected areas" which now equal the combined land areas of Western Europe. These areas, two-thirds of them in the Third World, have grown by eighty percent since 1970. Too often, however, pious declaration replaces pragmatic protection. For instance:

In many tropical areas - Sri Lanka is a case in point, fishermen daily dynamite and "mine" coral; this to supplement their incomes by using the lime-rich coral in the production of otherwise expensive, imported cement. The consequence is destruction of unique and irreplaceable resources, the growing erosion of coastal land and the destruction (not least) of beaches earning precious hard currency, through tourism, for many tropical island states. Yet the destruction of coral is illegal in Sri Lanka.

Regulation by itself is rarely adequate. To function, it must stand on three solid supports:

a)   Development of alternate income sources for those required to "stop doing" things destructive to our mutual ecology.

b)   Education, so people will understand and, in time, demand protection of their environments.

c)   Inspection and enforcement.

All three requirements are, in the developing world, mostly observed in the breach. No great suprise there.

The industrial nations, with vastly more resources, have begun enforcing their environmental and protection regulations mostly only in the past decade. In North America, examples of the failures of inspection and enforcement are still more apparent than models of ethical probity, ecological rectitude and community responsibility.

We can excuse the globe's poor (both governments and individual families), reduced to over-use and degradation of land (and thereby, plant and animal species) in their daily, hand-to-mouth struggle to survive another day, another week. They can only change as we provide them with the two resources they must have to alter their lives: opportunity and knowledge.

Not so with wealthy governments and transnational corporations. To watch these agencies squander plant and animal treasures we can never replace, is to enter a surreal world. A pauper, lighting his last bit of fuelwood with his last dollar bill, would more look rational.

Unfortunately, the currency of environmental treasure is not ours to burn: We've not even leased it from our children and theirs. We are, rather, custodians for them of the fundamental underpinnings of their lives.

In the field of global energy policy, one might add, we've been about as sensible as that fellow burning the last of his money for one final, tiny pool of light and heat. As we shall see, in the next chapter.

Chapter Seven

HOW TO SUMMON
THE ENERGY

A few hundred thousand years ago, "energy for survival" meant strong legs, to escape the sabre-toothed tiger. It meant, too, strong arms and backs to fight and kill the game needed for food. Sometime later, as early members of our species crossed the Mediterranean land bridge from Africa to Europe, priorities changed. Cleverness and ability to plan ahead became as vital as strength and speed: the "fire tender" who kept a few moss-wrapped, glowing coals alive during nomadic travel became vital. In Europe's harsh winters, no fire meant no survival. We are tomorrow's "keepers-of-the-flame."

We are already using or testing many forms of "renewable" energy, from human and animal muscle to wood, hydro (water) generated electricity, cattle dung, biogas, plant-generated energy, solar and tidal power, geothermal energy, wind power and nuclear breeder reactors. They are as tangible as those prehistoric coals. But our primary sources of energy - natural gas, coal, peat, oil, even conventional nuclear energy - are non-renewable; each relies on a finite resource base. Even in the field of renewable energy fuels (timber, plants, even dung) we very often use available supplies much faster than they can be replaced with existing policies.

In the Seventies, when western Canadian oil producers (in the province of Alberta) could not get the high prices they wanted from eastern Canada's industrial belt, they coined a half-jesting slogan which soon appeared on auto bumper stickers:

"Let the bastards freeze in the dark."

We'd invoke no such cynical curse on our children, or

theirs. Yet the sum of current global energy policy may inflict precisely that future on our global village. We need no research to understand the future's needs. They are simple and direct:

a) Energy supplies must be adequate to permit a minimum of three percent annual growth of GNP in all developing countries.

b) We need to develop aggressive and effective measures of fuel conservation and energy efficiency.

c) We must build public health factors into all our energy cost analyses.

d) We have to protect both our global biosphere, and our local and regional ecosystems from energy-produced pollution.

e) We have to share energy resources more fairly. At present, individuals in industrial nations use eighty times more energy than those in sub-Saharan Africa; one-quarter of the world's population, today, uses three-quarters of the planet's primary energy production.

Some context, and some perspective:

- In 1980, our global village used about ten "Terawatts" of energy - a terawatt (or 'TW') equals the energy released by burning about one billion tonnes of coal.

- If per capita energy consumption holds at today's rates, we'll need forty percent more by 2025 to cover population increase. But, if we equalize energy consumption and bring the Third World up to western energy use levels, we'll have to increase energy production by 550 percent in the next thirty-five years.

There's respectable, indeed overwhelming, rationale to bring energy consumption in developing countries more into line with Western consumption. Energy use is directly related to development and GNP. Lack of sufficient energy, to turn the coin over, means poverty. Some examples from 1984:

a) The world's "low income" nations, that year, used an average of four-tenths of a kilowatt of energy per person. Their average per capita GNP was $260.

b) The industrial world used about seven kilowatts of energy per person, and had a per capita GNP of $11,430.

70

In the industrial nations, that is, every individual benefited from the use of 17.5 times as much energy, and lived in an economy producing 43.9 times as much, per person, in goods and services.

Not only does easier access to energy mean more income in a direct, mathematical progression: there is actually an observable multiplier effect - (of two-and-a-half times, as we just saw, in 1984). Small wonder Third World nations are feeling both victimized, and determined to seek a more fair portion of the globe's energy.

How to do that?

Even with intense efforts in energy conservation and efficiency, any reasonable level of development in the Third World, combined with continuing development in the West, will likely see us using thirty-five terawatts annually forty years from now. That 3.5-fold increase over today's energy consumption would have unthinkable environmental consequences if we simply expanded our state-of-the-art energy production because we would have to:

Use 1.6 times as much oil each year, and:

a) Consume 3.4 times as much natural gas annually,

b) Burn five times as much coal as the 1980 level,

c) Increase nuclear power generation by thirty times over 1980 levels. This would mean installing a new nuclear power plant about every three days over the next forty years!

We can reduce those potential power needs by at least half: but it will take an energy efficiency revolution. No lesser goal is worth pursuing.

A high energy future for the world implies untenable risks:

- Climate change caused by the "greenhouse effect."
- Severe urban-industrial air pollution.
- Major environmental destruction and health hazards from acid rain.
- Appalling risks of nuclear accidents and radioactive contamination from waste disposal. (This not to mention the spiraling dangers of the spread of nuclear weapons, which often are directly tied to weapons-grade plutonium produced in nuclear power plants around the world.)

If, as seems certain unless we abandon current energy

patterns, we quadruple coal burning, increase oil consumption by 1.4, and double use of natural gas, we can assume "significant global warming" over the next thirty years. So what is "significant?"

It is an average temperature increase, globally, of from 1.5 to 4.5 degrees Celsius, as the carbon dioxide released from burning fossil fuels builds, which produces the "greenhouse effect" and traps solar heat inside our atmospheric envelope. So what? This:

Scientific modeling studies say this much change, even at the lower end of the forecasts, would raise sea levels from between one metre-plus to as much as eight metres (over the height of a three storey building). Low-lying coastal cities (often the most populous) and agricultural lands (usually the most fertile, in delta regions) would vanish under the world's oceans. No one can guess the economic, social and political disasters which would follow - just thirty years from now.

Will it happen? We can't be certain. How can we be sure? By carrying-on as we go, and risking the consequences. All a bit, you might observe, like crossing a busy superhighway, on foot, and blindfolded: this on the assumption the statistical risks will maybe be suspended for the moment. Not a terrific prescription for survival. Nor is technology going to be our saviour from this recipe for mutual destruction; we do not have any technology to remove carbon dioxide emission from fossil fuel burning. We can reduce sulphur and nitrogen emissions, and thus acid rain. But to avoid accelerating the greenhouse effect we simply have to stop multiplying our use of oil, gas, coal and the other fossil fuels - and especially coal.

Many observers cite the need for vast structural and economic changes to develop a "safe" energy future. They're right. But present knowledge shows the globe can have the development levels we need (allowing for a fifty percent drop in per capita energy use in the industrial states, and a thirty percent increase in the developing nations), if we use the most energy-efficient technologies and systems we already have and understand, and use them in every sector of our economies.

Tough? You bet. Not unlike the hundred-year-old philosopher who was asked if he found it very difficult to be lame, hard-of-hearing and handicapped by failing vision. "Not," he said, "when I consider the clear alternative." <u>We have no alternatives.</u>

We've already seen, over the past thirteen years in the industrial states, we can make industrial products with as much as a thirty-three percent reduction of energy used, per unit of production (make that a sixty percent reduction in Japan). To make those improvements universal, to allow continuing growth and development (without destroying the global society development should serve), we'll have to move more quickly. There's a lot to do. We must:

a) Vastly improve and extend monitoring and assessment of hazards.

b) Increase research dramatically - and globally.

c) Develop international - and internationally-accepted standards to reduce the emission and accumulation of noxious gases.

d) Plan and agree on strategies, now, to deal with the climate change already in train, and minimize damage from rising sea levels. A lot of today's complacent economists, planners and politicians are going to have very red faces - and very wet feet, if we don't plan the technological "dikes" we'll soon need.

The pursuit of more **energy efficiency** is our most urgent immediate goal.

Even today, about one third of global warming is caused, not by burning fossil fuels, but from other chemicals - chiefly the chlorofluocarbons used in refrigeration systems, aerosol sprays and plastics manufacture. These chemicals will cause half of all global warming forty years from now, if their use is not curbed. Aerosol tins powered by CFCs are already banned in several countries; the ban should be universal. The chemical industry, to ensure its own survival, should accelerate programmes to find industrial substitutes for chlorofluorocarbons, especially in blown plastics production, refrigeration and air conditioning.

All new development schemes, especially those hinged on bilateral or multilateral aid, or the participation of the IMF, World Bank or other international agencies, must begin to incorporate impact studies related to health, climate and environment - beginning with feasibility studies.

Similarly, the most energy-efficient and environmentally sound technologies should be fundamental to any new industrial or energy utility development, globally.

No one can project or estimate the global damage already done by acid rain. The World Health Organization estimated, in July, 1987, the health of 600 million people was at risk from this cause alone - as many people, that is, as the entire population of Europe.

In the U.S., a group of medical researchers and physicians has told the American Senate they now regard acid rain as the leading cause of lung cancer, after smoking.

In Europe, acid rain damage to forests and lakes may already be irreversible.

In Japan, there are studies showing crop losses in grain and rice production of up to thirty percent from acid rain.

We are sacrificing our forests, our lakes, our food production and the health - even the lives - of our children. Yet we can stop acid rain at a cost of two or three percent more on our electricity bills. That's all it would take.

We wouldn't long abide a neighbour firing random rifle bullets through the walls of our home:

Why do we allow the equally direct and intimate invasion of our communities, and our lungs, of wind-borne, transnational killers such as acid rain? Equally, why do we persist in firing those same shots through our neighbour's windows, with the puerile excuse we "need more research" to see whether the gun is loaded?

Similar riddles and contradictions of rational behaviour attend our development of nuclear energy. The world's most respected and conservative experts freely predict more Chernobyls, even without a further spread of nuclear generating stations. Opinion polls globally show ninety percent of us fear nuclear accidents; well over half the world's citizens say they do not believe the reassurances of the nuclear industry; they have cause:

Many recent revelations have shown consistent "cover-ups" (by both government agencies and industries) of nuclear hazards and of inadequate design, safety and monitoring procedures in atomic energy plants.

Even in terms of the most sterile economic arguments, divorced from the costs and risks of obvious hazards, the predicted advantages of nuclear power generation over conventional forms of power have evaporated with lower petroleum prices.

Few of us would light a brush fire beside our own homes if we lacked both the knowledge and the equipment to put it out, before we lost our home and belongings. Yet, with thousands of tonnes of radioactive waste now stockpiled from nuclear generating plants, we still do not know how, safely, to dispose of these most lethal poisons ever created.

There are now 366 operating nuclear power plants in the world; another 140 are in the active planning stage. The potential for tragedy increases with every new plant - and not just localized tragedy, as northwest Europe learned after Chernobyl.

Here's the blunt truth:

There can be no justification for building nuclear power plants until we can find bulletproof solutions to the lethal risks we are creating.

As a minimum, we have got to:

a) Have universal agreement on notification, internationally, of nuclear accidents and hazards, together with an effective surveillance and monitoring system.

b) Plan ahead for emergency response to the accidents we know we are going to have.

c) Establish international agreements on the transport and storage of radioactive materials across any national boundaries.

d) Develop international standards of training and licensing of the men and women operating our nuclear power plants.

e) Apply minimal safety standards, world-wide.

f) Develop global standards for radioactive waste storage.

g) Develop global standards for dismantling and decontamination of nuclear plants which are ending their span of productivity.

To turn from the macro to the micro challenges and problems of energy production:

About seventy percent of the developing world's population still depends on wood for fuel, heat, even light. The hazards are many and varied:

- Pneumonia death rates, especially among infants and children, are extremely high in societies where family huts are constantly filled with wood smoke from open, three-stone fires. In some areas (such as the highlands of Ethiopia) over half of all small children hospitalized are suffering severe burns, from falling into cooking fires.

-      More broadly, wood supplies are dwindling faster than they can be replaced in many areas. While villagers and farmers tend mostly to gather dead branches and twigs, Third World city dwellers often rely on timber cut from diminishing forest stocks and trucked to urban areas. As supplies shrink, prices rise:

In Ethiopia's capital city, Addis Ababa, many families have to spend as much as half their entire income on fuel for cooking, and to survive the cold nights at over three thousand metres above sea level.

There are solutions:

- Fast-growing varieties of fuelwood could be "farmed" on small lots, especially on hilly terrain where they would help retain soil moisture and prevent erosion.

- There are several models of "fuel-efficient" stoves being used throughout the Third World. Most can be built, at literally no cost, from mud-and-straw brick, baked in the sun. Most are at least four times as fuel efficient at the traditional, three-stone, open fire. One example:

When a fuel-efficient, mud-brick stove was used at a large feeding centre in Ethiopia, the cooking time to prepare a large pot of rice was reduced by four-and-a-half times; the fuel consumption was cut six times; and the food was cooked more thoroughly and more evenly.

-      Ethiopian technicians have developed a solar cooker for family use. It is simply a molded, parabolic mud dish, baked hard in the sun and covered in metal foil. This "solar dish" is adjustable according to the height of the sun, and has a hook on which to hang a cooking pot.

The solar cooker boils a litre of water in eight minutes, at no cost in fuel. But villagers, seeing the water boil with no

76

visible flame, fear the "evil spirit" or "magic" used in this glittering contraption. Moral: progress always depends on education; and on the creation of, not just acceptance, but demand at the grass roots level.

As of today, the development of renewable energy sources is at about the same stage of human, technological evolution as the stone axe, or of "slash and burn" farming.

About twenty-one percent of worldwide energy consumption today is from renewable sources. The remaining potential, especially in hydro power, is immense. Benefits would be stunning if, for example, neighbouring nations and regions developed hydro potential cooperatively, and shared those resources. The continuing development of "super conductors" is a particularly exciting prospect in this regard.

Solar power generation with photovoltaic cells now costs about $5 per "peak watt" as compared with $1 or $2 for conventional electricity. However that $5 figure is down from $600 a mere decade ago; it will soon reach the competitive price level. In the meantime, solar power is still cheaper, in remote areas, than construction of long-distance power grids or the importation of fuel.

In California, experience indicates wind-generated power will be competitive with conventional electricity within a decade.

Brazil produced ten billion litres of ethanol fuel alcohol, from sugar cane, in 1984. The cost was competitive with 1981 world oil prices. With a drop in petroleum prices, Brazil's advantage is that it still saves 60 percent of its former, hard currency costs of importing fuel for energy.

Even geothermal energy generation, tapping into the earth's subterranean furnaces, has increased fifteen percent in every recent year. No one knows the ultimate potential.

A great advantage of non-traditional and renewable energy systems:

They are mostly labour-intensive and best suited to small-scale, community or family enterprise. So they generate employment and, at the same time, are safe from international swings in prices, foreign exchange rates and security of supply.

We have most of the technology we need. The real hurdles are political and institutional. National energy policies must dramatically increase emphasis on renewable energy and experimental pilot projects. The means must be found to dynamite the log-jam of inertia and vested interest which prevents the giant electrical utilities from venturing into new systems, or accepting power supplied by smaller, less conventional systems.

There is only one acceptable power monopoly: It is the one "owned" by our children, and theirs, for whom we must guarantee an energy secure - and energy safe - future.

Ironically, by denying Third World families the benefit of our knowledge and help, we are accelerating their spiral into poverty and guaranteeing their inefficient use of the few resources they possess. Energy provides a classic case in point:

A rural mother in India, Nigeria or Brazil, cooking her family's meal in an earthen pot, over a three-stone fire, uses eight times as much energy as her neighbour, using a metal pot on a gas-fired stove.

In the Third World many families obtain their only light from a string or wick, dipped into a pot of palm oil, or a jar of kerosene. For their children, studying school lessons in the tropics, where darkness falls at six in the evening, year round, the traditional oil or kerosene lamp gives only one-fiftieth the illumination of one 100-watt light bulb. A kerosene-dipped wick, to be explicit, has the same illumination one would get from a two-watt bulb, if you can imagine one. Yet the kerosene or oil lamp uses the same amount of energy as that consumed by the 100-watt bulb.

The industrial nations would likely approach a state verging on civil war or revolution were their citizens suddenly forced to pay fifty times more for equivalent energy use to light their homes.

Another note about the economics of genuinely efficient energy:

A study in Brazil examined the cost of producing truly energy- efficient products with current technology - from refrigerators and autos to street lights and electric motors. Total investment (much of which would be recovered) was estimated at four billion dollars.

However, the investment of four billion, it turned out, would save Brazil $19 billion over fourteen years, through reduced need to build a huge network of new power generating stations.

Every nation should require "energy labelling" of all appliances. People do behave rationally, when they are informed, and given choices.

Energy "book-keeping" is essential in every sphere of activity, as are "energy audits" of all commercial and industrial enterprises. Current experience proves the pragmatic and immediate economic benefits of this system to industry. In future, enterprises which fail in this area will become as redundant as the makers of buggy whips and bustles.

At the moment, transport accounts for up to sixty percent of all petroleum use in industrial nations. We've seen remarkable improvements in fuel efficiency in this decade. But we know the current average consumption (of one hundred kilometres per ten litres of fuel) could be cut by a further fifty percent in the next twelve years with sustained effort. The savings in air pollution alone would be monumental.

We can probably assume new and safer, more efficient forms of energy in our future, if we have a future:

Hydrogen energy; safe, renewable, nuclear fusion energy (which does not produce the plutonium and other terrible, radioactive poisons common to our present "fission" nuclear plants) and "breeder" reactors; mile-long, solar panels "parked" in space to relay 24-hour energy from sun to earth: all are possible, as is a gigantic harnessing of the limitless heat locked in the earth's core. But those potentials have about as much value to that Third World mother we discussed, with her three-stone fire, as does a parachute in a cupboard at home, to someone thrown from an airplane.

By using the technology we know about now, by intensifying our pursuit of renewable energy and energy conservation, we can buy the time we need, until that global, energy parachute is delivered. If we fail to do these things, our landing may be very rough - and very soon.

Chapter Eight

ENVIRONMENTALLY RESPONSIBLE
INDUSTRY

Environmentalists have, for many years, had a love/hate relationship with industrialists. The global village must have industrial technology to solve our environmental problems - and industrial production to fuel the engine of development. But, beginning in the Fifties, industry was seen as the enemy, the Great Destroyer of our ecosphere.

Until the middle of this century, London, England took pride in its nickname, "The Big Smoke"; it had implied the concentration of industry, wealth and power for two centuries. But with the Fifties came London's "killer smog" and an epidemic of pollution-triggered deaths from respiratory failure. Industry wasn't the only villain, of course. The smoke from a million coal-fired household stoves and fireplaces added mightily to the accretion of deadly smoke.

Our awareness of pollution costs grew with the Los Angeles smogs, the "death" of Lake Erie, the profound degradation of major European rivers including the Elbe, the Meuse and the Rhine. The late Fifties brought us the epidemic of mercury poisoning in Minamata, Japan, and in northwest Ontario, in Canada. We began hearing horror stories of asbestosis in plant workers and lead poisoning in urban children.

As our understanding of pollution hazards grew through the late Fifties and Sixties, the battle lines were drawn:

On one side, environmentalists calling for the scalps of polluters; on the other, industrialists who had been accustomed to being seen as social benefactors - providing employment and wealth - but now portrayed as virtual criminals, and unfeeling exploiters. At the extremes, environmentalists saw industrial managers as near-monsters; corporate leaders viewed the environmentalists as ill-informed anarchists, trying to destroy the benefits of industrialization indiscriminately.

"Zero Growth" and "Small Is Beautiful" were the legends on battle flags. Conservationists looked like implacable foes of all progress to industry; but to those intent on preserving our planet, the globe's industrial plant was a juggernaut, remorselessly grinding nature and people alike under its giant wheels. Both views, as we know now, were as wrong as they were simplistic.

Industry can enhance our ecosphere as easily as degrade it. Environmentalists can and do work with industry, as must we all.

Industrial production exploded in the two decades following 1950; we produce seven times more in total goods and services than we did thirty-five years ago; this although growth seems now to have stabilized at about three percent annually.

Developing countries, with almost no industry at all when they gained independence after World War Two, now account for about twelve percent of global manufacturing. (India is now the world's ninth-ranking industrial power.) Third world nations, though, are less than halfway to the goal of twenty-five percent of world production adopted by the United Nations Industrial Development Organization in Lima, in 1975.

New industries in developing nations are not always good news. The bulk of them are the capital-intensive, heavy industries - in the fields of chemicals, metal products, machinery and equipment - which are, generally, the worst polluters. Third World countries, more seriously, usually lack the expertise and resources needed to assess environmental risk, to monitor manufacturing and to enforce adequate pollution controls.

There's been a considerable and visible environmental improvement and pollution reduction, especially in industrial states. (Witness the clean-up of London's "killer smog" and of the Thames.) But we are still losing ground in many areas:

- Fertilizer and sewerage run-off are increasing (the

latter exacerbated by mushrooming populations in Third world cities); so we have more fish kill globally, more poisoned water and increasing destruction of plant life, in our seas and on land.

- Atmospheric levels of sulphur and nitrogen oxides are rising in many areas. Lead pollution is endemic in Third world cities, where emission controls on autos, trucks and buses are non-existent; and most vehicles, kept on the roads twice as many years on average as in the West, are poorly maintained.

In many cities in the developing world, air pollution is already worse than any experienced in industrial nations in the Fifties or Sixties.

- Chemical pollution has spread to every corner of the globe. Heavy metals and other toxins have been found in the most remote and isolated birds, animal and marine species of the arctic and antarctic.

Fortunately the experience of the past two decades has shown us how to attack these problems. Moreover, we have learned pollution controls are good business and good economics. Even ignoring the vast savings in health and lives, the plant and animal species saved, pollution-free industry almost invariably earns or saves more money than it costs. It's noteworthy, for example, that the only steel companies doing reasonably well in the current world price slump are those which have made themselves the most efficient, environmentally. Another example:

- About half Canada's eighty pulp and paper plants have installed, or plan to install, environmentally safe anaerobic treatment of their effluent discharge. The system costs from three to four million dollars per plant and requires annual operating costs of about $500,000. But these anaerobic systems generate savings of one million dollars annually. So after allowing for operating costs, the new treatment schemes generate a half-million dollars yearly, which repays their installation costs in six to eight years; after that, they produce a $500,000 annual profit.

- As noted, cleaning-up acid rain would add only from two to three percent to average electricity billings. Public opinion polls show most consumers would happily pay that cost. But there also are actual dollar benefits involved.

In the northeastern U.S. for instance, it's estimated a full clean-up will cost from six to seven billion dollars a year; but the annual costs, in this same area, of corrosion damage caused by acid rain is nine billion dollars (this without even taking health costs into account). Add to that lakes and fisheries destroyed, tourist revenue lost, a maple sugar industry being decimated annually by acid rain damage, and still-to-be-estimated losses in forestry industries.

In hard fact, the "environmental industry sector" has become the globe's most certain growth industry. In Canada, by way of example:

- There are now 200,000 workers employed in this sector.

- The environment industry sector employs twelve times more people than those engaged in coal mining - twice as many as all the workers employed in motor vehicle production - forty percent more than the total jobs in every segment of the textile and clothing industry.

Too often still, environmental controls are "reactive" rather than "proactive." We identify a problem, often only when it has become critical, and "fix it."

Every such case of crisis management is a public demonstration of failure.

In truth, our spasm-response, fire-fighting system of pollution abatement is, by vast proportions, the most expensive possible method we could adopt. It is about as sensible as paying Super Concorde fares for a subway trip to the office.

Let's examine the scale of growth we're going to need - and need to monitor and control it environmentally:

- If we sought to raise Third world consumption of manufactured goods to sustainable industrial nation levels, to create markets, raise living standards and sustain world development, global industrial output would have to increase 2.6 times over current production. That's just for now.

- Given expected population growth, we'll need from five to ten times more industrial production than today's by the time our global village census levels-off, fifty to seventy-five years from now.

84

(Much of this expansion must occur within the Third World. This not least because the youthful "population bulge" in developing countries will soon throw hundreds-of-millions of young people onto the job market; they cannot be employed in agriculture - there are no jobs.)

To put those numbers into perspective, remember we have increased global industrial production forty times, in just the past thirty-five years. We need the projected growth we've discussed to build prosperity in the Third World, as well as to create stable markets for Western development. The questions:

-    Have we the basic resources for such growth?

-    Can we grow so much, and still protect our environment?

The answers to both are, "yes." But, a very qualified yes.

We must begin by helping developing nations to learn from our mistakes. No developing nations can muster the resources to, "industrialize now, and fix the problems later" as has happened in the West. Nor, given the crippling exponential curves built into pollution, would they anyway have the time.

Start, too, with a critical look at much of our "conventional wisdom." Such goals in manufacturing - for example, "the economies of scale" - are no longer necessarily a hallmark of efficiency and profitability:

New communications, information and process control technology permit small-scale, decentralized industries widely scattered across a country. Clearly, such dispersion reduces impact on local environments and makes controls easier at individual sites. Further, small-scale processing of raw materials is more labour intensive - so less energy intensive and, thereby, less polluting. Labour intensive industry, as we've noted, is what the Third World needs. One more point:

Small-scale industries will cater to the needs of the local and regional population; their products are far more likely to be "appropriate" to their consumers.

So what about the availability of the resources we'll need to grow? Some examples from our contemporary experience:

a)   Between 1973 and 1989, Japan reduced the amount of

85

raw material used in each unit of production by sixty percent - whether that unit was an auto, a tv set, or a railway car. That reduction, moreover, took place while overall manufacturing output was growing steadily.

b)   In the USSR, industrial chemical production rose seventy percent from 1975 to 1980. In the same period, total consumption of fresh water by that industry stayed constant.

c)   Older, "traditional" pulp and paper mills use about 180 cubic metres of fresh water to produce every tonne of pulp. Mills built since the early Seventies use only seventy cubic metres, a reduction of about sixty percent. Still newer methods, where water is cleansed and re-circulated, could bring water consumption down to twenty or thirty cubic metres per tonne of pulp made - one-ninth the volume formerly needed.

d)   In steel mills, anywhere from eighty to two hundred tonnes of water are needed to produce a tonne of crude steel. But "closed," re-circulation systems could reduce this to only about three tonnes - just the amount lost through evaporation.

Resource efficiency is possible. It is being practiced now in many sectors where its pragmatic potential has been tested and accepted. New materials - ceramics, rare metals and metal alloys, high-performance plastics, and new composites are now playing a significant role in both energy and resource conservation.

Biotechnology has a major role to play:

-    More and more, plant-derived energy (as from Brazil's sugar cane) offers a fully renewable energy source and reduction of fossil fuel burning.

-    Research already promises biologically-based, cleaner, more efficient processes in industrial sectors which are heavy polluters.

-    Other research may soon give us cheap, safe ways to eliminate hazardous liquid wastes. One firm has patented a genetically-engineered bacteria to "eat" and digest petroleum from marine oil spills.

-    "Giant bacteria" up to 1.5 centimetre long, were found on the sea floor in the Gulf of Mexico in early 1990. These creatures thrive on a diet of hydrogen sulphide, the major by-product of ocean floor oil seepage. In the process, the bacteria break down the poisonous hydrogen sulphide into much less hazardous sulphur and water.

Satellite imagery, now vital through weather observations to global agriculture, could help us make the best and most efficient use of planet-wide resources - this by monitoring and assessing long-term trends in climate, erosion, plant cover, and marine pollution.

One of the most dramatic and exciting areas of genetic engineering holds the possibility of plants which could literally absorb the nitrogen they need from the air. Such a development would have a profound impact on the world's fertilizer industry. It would also reduce the globe's burden of agricultural pollution immensely.

Our first step is to establish ground rules and benchmarks:

Governments, industry and the public must be equally involved. Trans-boundary pollution must be regulated. Every nation must accept responsibility to avoid damaging its neighbours, responsibility to compensate for trans-border damage, and to provide full access to all available remedial measures.

Governments must beware policies which, through direct and indirect subsidies, effectually encourage resource depletion, and pollution. Even our water comes with a price tag: Resource depletion and degradation, even when they are "written between the lines," are an integral part of every governmental and corporate balance sheet. Those costs must be part of our explicit, public records. Full and accurate environmental bookkeeping is vital to the understanding we need for survival.

Small and medium-sized business are still the world's major employers and producers. Lacking the resources of the multinationals, they are also our worst polluters. Major corporations and governments must share pollution and resource control technology with small business. Metal working, leather tanning and dying, printing, machine tool manufacture, even photo processing are among the worst offenders in our global village. Governments, too, can and should encourage cooperative, industry-wide preventive and remedial programmes within each small-scale industrial sector. These efforts could include joint use of pollution control facilities, recycling equipment and waste treatment plants.

We need infinitely more study of the chemical genies we've been releasing from nature's storehouse, and creating artificially. A lot of them are Frankensteins. Consider:

- There are between 70,000 and 80,000 chemicals now in the global marketplace - and that means in our environment.

- We are putting from 1,000 to 2,000 new chemicals on our sales shelves, every year.

- Of the 65,725 most commonly used chemicals, we have proper health and environmental risk data for only one pesticide in ten, and one drug in six (this according to a study by the U.S. Research Council). More than five hundred chemicals had been banned with respect to both production and sale, in the West, by 1986. Many of them are still being made in, or exported to, developing nations. Third world nations almost universally lack the import controls, inspection facilities, technical expertise, human resources and data needed to control these practices.

Beyond research on existing products, every nation should ban the production and distribution of any chemical or compound until it has been proved safe. Every scrap of information about hazardous chemicals must be made public.

Chemical manufacturers, like the pharmaceutical makers, should be required to make every effort to ensure the end users, whether of pesticides, industrial solvents or other products, will not misunderstand safe handling instructions or the dangers of misuse. There were, remember, 10,000 deaths from pesticide poisoning in the Third World, last year.

The same standards applied within industrial states must be applied equally to all chemical exports, or creation of offshore manufacturing facilities. Call this a new form of extra-territoriality if you will. But it does not represent an effort to influence or dictate-to other nations; it is, rather, simple recognition we are our brothers' and sisters' keepers, as they are ours.

A note to put the responsibility of the industrial nations into perspective:

In 1984 the world produced between 325 and 375 million tonnes of hazardous wastes. Only five tonnes was produced in all the newly industrialized and developing nations of the Third World.

We know we are going to have more disastrous industrial accidents and break-downs:

- One thousand died when liquid gas storage tanks exploded in Mexico City.

- Two thousand died at Bhopal.

- Then there was Sevesso, with scores of miscarried pregnancies and infants born malformed.

- The chemical plant fire at Basle in Switzerland, in November 1986, caused massive fish kills in waterways as far downstream as The Netherlands.

There will be more. No week has passed in this decade without a potentially catastrophic "close call" somewhere in the world.

So the global village needs a linked network of risk assessment, monitoring, and "environmental fire brigades." Factory workers and people in the vicinity of chemical plants must be fully informed both of dangers and of appropriate, life-saving measures they can take in emergencies.

In the industrial nations, drivers are fined if their auto turn signals and brake lights don't work. But we permit corporate secrecy within the factories constituting many of our most lethal health risks   - be they nuclear generating plants, explosives factories, or chemical manufacturers.

Both industry and governments must be involved in risk assessment and identification of hazardous operations - **and full public disclosure of those facts.**

National and international trade unions, too, have a fundamental responsibility to provide us with risk data, and to inform their neighbours of unsafe materials and practices.

It is the workers (be they lathe operators or chemists), when all is said, who are at the cutting edge of pollution risk. They perform the acts, manufacture the compounds which can threaten us all - not least themselves and their children.

Each of them, therefore, has a community

responsibility which far transcends their loyalty to any employer. Industrial employees have no more right than the war criminals of World War Two to claim they are, "only following orders." Clearly the suppression of information vital to community safety is a social crime - often with consequences which dwarf the carnage of all the serial killers and mass murderers of history. **But society at large must protect workers who give us the information from the reprisals of corporations which are inflicting damage on our environment, and on our children.**

It concerns us all.

If any of us failed to warn a blind man he was about to walk into the path of a speeding truck, we might well be charged with criminal negligence, or manslaughter. Imagine yourself on a jury considering the act of any government, any industry, any individual, suppressing life-saving facts about lethal chemical toxins.

Consider, again, the ten thousand dead, every year, from pesticide poisoning. Knowledge is power. The power of understanding has got to be shared, globally, if we are to survive to grow - and grow to survive.

Chapter Nine

EXPLODING CITY POPULATIONS

In ten years, almost half of us all will be living in urban areas. The increase is most dramatic in the developing nations, where urban population increased ten times between 1920 and 1980 - from 100 million to one billion. Today, one in every three of us lives in a city or town; one in ten lives in a city with a population of one million or more.

This isn't all a result of simple population increase. More than half the rising urban population results from people migrating to cities from the countryside, looking for jobs, housing, education for their children.

Growth rates have been slowing - from an average of 5.2 percent annual increase in the late Fifties to about 3.4 percent yearly in this decade. But over the next fifteen years, we'll have to increase our global capacity to provide urban services - shelter, water, sewerage facilities, schools, urban transport, roads and the rest, by sixty-five percent. Nor are we, realistically, talking here about "merely" expanding existing city infrastructures. In truth, most Third World cities, today, have services adequate to serve only a fraction of their existing populations.

In developing nations, most housing occupied by the armies of the poor is decrepit, to give it the rosiest description possible. (For tens-of-millions of families, "home" is a cardboard shanty, a scrap-wood lean-to huddled against another building, a length of empty sewer pipe not yet used by local contractors, a ragged tent, a corrugated tin shack, a palm thatch hut likely to collapse in the first monsoon rain - maybe just a ditch or some space to sleep on the bare earth or pavement.)

Civic buildings in most Third World countries are in an acute stage of decay. Where water and sewerage systems exist, they are usually best described as Dickensian; installed by colonial rulers maybe one hundred years ago, they were designed for populations of perhaps one-twentieth today's and are, anyway, well past their maintainable life span. Ancient, corroded-and-leaking water lines mean reduced pressure, which allows contaminated ground water and sewerage to seep into municipal water systems which may already be contaminated - most commonly, with lead.

In the same way, public transport is overcrowded, overused and under-maintained. The hallmark of Third world urban transit is the sight of youths and men clinging to the sides of buses or trams, hanging from the windows of commuter trains - even sitting nonchalantly atop bulging railway passenger cars.

So, too, with roads, communal latrines, neighbourhood water taps or wells.

The results are direct and utterly predictable:

-       Acute respiratory diseases are common, and commonly fatal. In many regions it is "normal" to find one hundred percent, severe infestation of children by intestinal parasites. Add those diseases most directly linked to overcrowding, to unsafe water and poor sanitation - cholera and dysentery, typhoid and hepatitis, polio and whooping cough - all are usually endemic. In the shanty settlement housing - up to half or more of most Third world cities - **one child in four will likely die in its first five years.**

-       In China, lung cancer rates in the largest cities are from four to seven times higher than the national average - and this in the country with the highest global, per capita use of tobacco (in rural as well as urban settings). The reason: industrialization has dramatically increased air pollution. (Remember those U.S. studies discussed earlier: acid rain may be the second-ranking contributor to lung cancer.)

- **Sixty percent of Calcutta's population suffers from pneumonia, bronchitis or other respiratory disease linked directly to air pollution.**

(There are about ten million people in Calcutta's metropolitan area. So in the environs of this one Asian city, count six million victims of air pollution - a number twice the total population of Albania - more than the entire citizenry of Denmark, Haiti, Finland or the Dominican Republic, in just one Third World city. Now consider the human consequences of exploding, Third World urban populations.)

- In all of India, precisely eight cities and towns have full sewage treatment facilities. Another 209 communities have partial systems and treatment. But 2,902 urban communities have no sewage systems at all. On the Ganges River alone, there are 114 communities, each of more than 50,000 population, dumping untreated sewerage into that "holy" river.

(For context, again, note the city of Montreal, Canada, dumps its raw sewage, every day, into the St. Lawrence River.)

The problems of cities in the developing nations are fiercely exacerbated by a lack of municipal resources. This problem has several causes:

a) Bureaucratic structures set in place by the European colonial powers never envisaged the stupendous growth of cities in Asia, Africa and Latin America. But these entirely inappropriate structures remain, largely unchanged, in the vastly different (too often, "indifferent") world we have, forty years after those colonies gained independence.

b) Many developing nations have copied Western urban systems and structures, assuming them to be the "most advanced" and therefore most efficient. Usually these role models have proven woefully unsuitable in a Third World setting. Like wine, some Western political institutions and traditions, it develops, "do not travel well."

c) Most fundamentally, municipal governments in developing nations rarely ever have the financial or political clout of city governments in the West. Invariably, most power (and this includes the vital power to levy taxes) is the sole prerequisite of the central, national government. In most cases, policing is provided by a national force, as are urban transport, commuter transport, social services and education.

(When Sri Lanka instituted directly-elected "local councils" in 1980, urban council members soon found they could not purchase so much as a single light bulb for their offices, without reference to the national Member of Parliament responsible for their area.)

There are exceptions. In China, urban councils have very considerable power - power reflected in an almost combative spirit of inter-urban competition which has contributed greatly to regional development and, ironically, to urban pollution as well.

The clear conclusion:

Third World cities need infinitely more power - to levy taxes, to organize and plan social services and infrastructure, if they are even to begin to meet the challenges now in place - let alone those of the next thirty years. The industrial nations must help - by providing both funds and expertise. In many cases, as proved by experience, the best and most pragmatic help will come through small, community-based cooperative movements and the efforts of neighbourhood-level, indigenous non-governmental organizations. These latter are especially effectual in planning and organizing health and social services, developing nutritional and sanitary schemes in shanty-towns, encouraging immunization, breast-feeding and the use of life-saving oral rehydration therapy for children suffering from diarrhea. But to begin, they need a measure of external support and encouragement - a "leg up."

Historically, cities dominate the economies of their nations. They attract innovative technology and industry which later may trickle-down to smaller centres. It's this urban position of economic leadership which draws job seekers from smaller communities and rural areas. In the West, this has led in turn to large increments in urban resources, to serve these growing populations. Not so in the developing world.

As we've noted, urban growth is slowing somewhat - and both decentralized industrial development and the growth of small enterprises can help relieve the pressures on our cities. But they are already in trouble, and the troubles are going to get worse. They cannot be addressed until the central governments of developing nations act to greatly strengthen local administrations. Industrial nations and international agencies need to encourage this essential change.

Paradox: one of the greatest economic strengths of developing nations' cities is under siege:

From one-third to one-half the employable populations of most Third World cities are, officially, "unemployed." Yet a host of these people work in the "informal sector" - a kind of "grey market" - providing very large fractions of the necessary goods and services to their cities. From fruit vending and roadside umbrella and bicycle repairs to house-building and tailoring, this underground work force both maintains itself and contributes, vitally, to the life of the city. But lacking licenses and any "formal existence," these small entrepreneurs are constantly vulnerable to greedy and corrupt officials, to bureaucratic harassment, and, without the protection of official recognition and stable price structures, to the lotteries of economic swings.

Third World governments would serve their citizens well by supporting this informal economic sector. At present, most governments view and treat such efforts, whether in community self-help or private enterprise, with attitudes ranging from active antagonism at worst, to benign neglect at best.

Until changes are made in the institutional attitudes toward this army of servants, security guards, unregistered factory workers, peddlars and the rest, they will go on in their endeavors; they will also go on mostly working from twelve to sixteen hours daily, seven days a week. Their problem is not lack of work - it's paucity of pay. So long as they remain outside mainstream wage and working regulations, nothing will improve for them - or for their cities, where they could and should be economy-building consumers and nation-building taxpayers.

Drastic - more accurately, revolutionary - change is needed in the provision of homes to the Third World's urban poor. For starters:

a)   The millions living in illegal urban settlements must be guaranteed tenure, given secure titles and provided basic municipal services, including safe water and latrines.

b)   The land and other resources people need to build homes - or make their present hovels habitable, must be found and made available.

c)   New and properly serviced housing areas must be prepared for the future influx of yet more families. If they, like those who preceded them, are left to "fend for themselves," the consequences will be disastrous - no less for their national economies than their immediate families.

d)   "Storefront" neighbourhood counselling is needed in every Third world city, to advise people on health, sanitation, housing, legal rights; and to explain how they can deal, with dignity, with the political and bureaucratic structures and strictures in their community.

e) Intensive effort should be devoted to encouraging small-scale "cottage" workshops and industries in shanty-towns and marginal housing areas. New disposable income will encourage people to improve their homes and surroundings. Microcosmic "local" enterprise is often the most efficient; labour is available - the market is outside the door - transport and distribution costs are nil - and the ubiquitous, profit-stealing, Third World "middleman" is eliminated.

f) Governments in developing nations must exercise firmer control over land speculators, who often "freeze" property urgently needed for housing, in hopes of future bonanzas.

g) "Urban agriculture" should be encouraged and assisted, whether by way of commercial market gardening to serve city populations, or individual, family vegetable gardens. Every Third world city has considerable plots of unused land which could be turned to this purpose; this not least in a "green belt" around cities which could encompass new housing estates, fuel-timber plantations, and food crops for both families and markets.

h) Solid waste disposal on a large scale is an almost ungovernable problem in Third World cities; this, ironically, in cultures where virtually everything is recycled at the street-stall-level of economic activity: vegetables and tea are wrapped in paper sacks made from yesterday's court transcripts, mail, or school examination papers; throw-away cigarette lighters are refilled by hypodermic; broken plastic utensils mend umbrellas or sandals tomorrow. There's a lesson here, from their least advantaged citizens, for the governments of the developing world:

Most Third World municipal governments lack the resources to collect and recycle all city waste. But such governments should observe the communities of squatter-scavengers living on the rim of every major Third World garbage dump - earning their living from hand-sorting waste for useful artifacts. Community cooperatives could multiply this chain of recycling and, at the same time, vastly reduce the waste pollution of cityscapes.

This is not just a fable applicable exclusively to the grinding poverty of Bombay or Mexico City. In an affluent suburb of Toronto, scores of people gather every weekend at "sales" held at the municipal garbage dump. There, whole families happily scavenge, pay for and cart-off furniture and other oddments they take home to recycle and repair. Virtue is rewarded, the municipality makes a profit and the volume of landfill garbage is reduced markedly.

In the meantime, advice and assistance in matters of health and sanitation is more urgent than words can express for the folk who, literally, live in garbage and its noxious by-products with their families. In the industrial world, we needed an urban sociologist, Jane Jacobs, to remind us cities are merely clusters of villages - adjacent neighbourhoods; they can survive and serve their residents only to the degree they develop and foster pride, dignity and community identity. Sure, we may leave the urban villages where we live, each morning, and "commute" to some other village cluster, downtown, to earn our bread. But the atavistic, gregarious, stories-around-the-evening-fire, tribal needs endure - as much in Manhattan or Rio, or Tokyo, as in Lagos or Calcutta. It should come as little surprise, in the industrial world, that our highest suicide rates are in the sterile, anonymous boxes of city high rise apartments.

The most exciting of all self-help urban ventures in the developing nations have sprung from *within* small communities, and been fueled by a shared sense of need, a communal agreement on goals.

It is in our own "communities," be they family, tribal, neighbourhood, that we each develop our notions of identity and of purpose and pride. All of those, with the encouragement of our neighbours, can lead to hope. As Burke also remarked,

"Where there is no hope, there can be no endeavour."

Curiously, there may be more sense of community, of unity and shared experience, in the shanty towns of Third World cities than in their "embassy rows." We'd best stop the efforts to ignore or uproot those fragile tendrils of future growth. Instead, we should nourish, cultivate and treasure the richest resources in our global village:

Initiative, ingenuity, improvisation, ambition, determination, and finally, the **hope of improvement** which can, alone, sustain endeavor. The world's urban poor demonstrate those qualities, every waking moment. They deserve some encouragement - even some help. Best it come from those of us, their neighbours, whose fates are tied so closely to theirs.

Will that be tough? Certainly, but, not when one considers the clear alternative.

Will it require change? Absolutely. Edmund Burke, again:

"A state without the means of change is without the means of its conservation."

Chapter Ten

OUR SHARED PERILS
AT SEA AND IN SPACE

The realities of the globally-shared facets of our planet - our interdependent world economy, as well as our mutual resources - space, the seas, and the polar regions, have made national sovereignty about as defensible as the Maginot Line or the "house of straw" built by the Three Little Pigs.

No fortress philosophy or bunker mentality can save any nation from the consequences of the illness of any of these shared and essential organs of our planet's life force. Neither can any nation state, acting alone, protect our atmosphere, our oceans, our polar lands.

We shall monitor, assess, develop and manage them together, or succumb, individually, and as a community of nations, to their degradation.

Even our weather is, literally and directly, "born-of-the-seas"   - from the trillions of photoplankton producing fresh oxygen, to the tides and heat exchange from the atmosphere in day-and-night cycles. Yet we continue to degrade the seas, which protect our climatic stability and, therefore, our crops and lives; and we go on messing with the atmosphere, which alone shields us - and our seas - from the ultra-violet assaults of the sun.

For centuries we've regarded our seas as boundless, able to absorb any punishment, any volume of pollution we inflicted on them. Now we know they cannot. We relied on the seas to cleanse our rivers and coasts; they cannot. We thought the oceans' harvests of fish a bottomless well of food; they are not. We thought ourselves puny creatures in the face of the vast oceans covering forty-five percent of the globe - impotent to affect or even disturb their grand design. We are not puny:

Our technology, and its waste, can make our seas and their skin, the atmosphere, sicken and die. Already, both are weak; soon they could be too ill to respond to treatment.

For centuries, we've used our rivers to carry first human, then industrial wastes away to the oceans. That left the rivers to flush themselves clean, at least for a time.

But the oceans have nowhere to unload their waste. They have become a series of interconnected, closed, sewage lagoons or tanks, however vast. Plastic garbage wastes have even been found washed ashore on the coasts of Antarctica.

The twenty-five percent of the globe's surface covered by fresh water contributes, minute-by-minute, to the growing pollution of our oceans. Sediment from our great rivers such as the Amazon can be found 2,000 kilometres from coastal waters. Deposits of heavy metals, petroleum, and chemical organochlorines, much of them from river estuaries, have been found in all our oceans.

During the period between the Fifties and the Seventies, our seas were bombarded by fallout from nuclear tests. This form of pollution, with consequences no one can forecast, has been magnified, year by year, by continuing disposal, in our oceans, of "low level" radioactive wastes.

Our seas are under assault, too, from both airborne pollutants and, more directly, from our ocean transport systems.

It's now estimated the total volume of oil spilled annually from tankers alone totals 1.5 million tonnes. Despite international treaties and national maritime regulations, most offenders escape either detection or penalty. We could fix that.

With satellite surveillance and modern communication, pollution can be traced to its source, and the owners/operators of that source held to account. Not least, these polluters should be publicly identified. A period of time in the "stocks" of the mass media would have a salutary effect on persistent polluters.

Satellites can be used to assist in developing a realistic inventory of our marine resources, and to track changes in the maritime environment. As with political public opinion polls, the emphasis, in the case of observing our aquatic environment, should be on the observation and study of "trends." Individual problems and "hot spots" must be identified, pursued and remedied. But it is through full understanding of developing changes alone we can organize and cooperate on long term preventive and remedial measures.

Over-fishing is as serious an ecological threat as pollution. Ninety-five percent of the world's fish harvest is taken from the continental shelves off our major coasts: all of it is now threatened by over-harvesting our fish. This isn't a nebulous, vague concern for the future. Witness recent history and experience:

Several of the world's major fisheries have collapsed under the burden of over-fishing. These include:

- The anchovy fisheries off Peru,
- Many of the North Atlantic herring stocks, and
- The California sardine harvest.

Elsewhere, in rich fisheries off the coast of West Africa, in the Gulf of Thailand and on the Grand Banks off Newfoundland, heavy fishing has caused dramatic changes in the proportions of various fish species. No one knows what the consequences will be.

The existing Law of The Sea Convention has helped some. With two hundred-mile national limits off coastlines, an extra thirty-five percent of our seascape has come under the control of individual nations. But many lack even the resources to monitor activity within their "coastal waters." (Even some wealthy industrial nations such as Canada utterly lack the means of patrolling their entire coastal waters.) Enforcement of national regulations, without close scrutiny of all activity in "national waters," is, in Shelley's words, as much to be relied-upon, "as summer's snow."

Most developing nations also lack either the capital or the expertise to use their expanded zones of interest for their own benefit. This situation won't change until the international development banks and other development agencies build programmes to help developing nations create the institutions, expertise and facilities they lack to protect their fisheries.

The wealthier nations are benefiting from the Law of the

Sea: in the Northwest Atlantic, for example, the catch of "long-range" fishing vessels from Europe dropped from over two million tonnes in 1974 to about a quarter-million tonnes in 1983. In the same period, the United States and Canada increased their "take" from these fisheries to over ninety percent of the total catch, from a level of less than fifty percent.

At the same time, however, the "industrial-strength" long-range, Japanese and European fisheries fleets continue to take some five million tonnes of fish off the shores of developing nations which are less able either to harvest their own resources, or enforce their protection. This century's "privateers" are huge fishing trawlers.

Off West Africa, by way of example, over half the annual catch is still captured by these sophisticated, long-range convoys of modern trawlers.

Third World countries are thus losing their national treasure through lack of maritime resources, and of processing and marketing facilities and skills, as well as their absolute inability to control the activities of marauding, foreign fishing fleets.

Small, Third World, island nations are the greatest potential victims of this modern version of exploitation. An early future scenario involving political instability is far from improbable within such poor nations deprived of the income and food they need for bare survival.

The industrial fishing states, in effect, have begun colonizing the seas in addition to land resources.

Even the current moratorium on whaling may be too little, and is clearly on the cusp of being too late. As for "too little":

-    Conservation groups believe, with considerable logic, the Treaty caveat permitting the catch of whales "for scientific purposes" provides a loophole for whaling nations. If the International Whaling Commission fails to more stringently supervise permissions for "scientific" whaling, it will soon lose any credibility.

As for "too late":

-    Even a cessation of whaling leaves the world with the prospect we will see no substantial increases in the population of endangered groups of the whale species for at least seventy-five years.

Efforts are underway to reduce maritime pollution. The London Dumping Convention of 1975 prohibits dumping "extremely dangerous substances" including high-level radioactive wastes. Additionally,

-    "Somewhat less noxious substances" may be dumped "only by prior special permit," and

-    All other substances may be dumped only with permission from the appropriate national authorities.

Still, until 1983, Belgium, Switzerland, The Netherlands and The United Kingdom continued dumping "low-level radioactive wastes" in international waters off the coast of Spain. Since 1983 there has been a de facto, but unofficial, moratorium on this dumping - and general agreement - informally again - disposal should await evidence it is environmentally safe.

Although it wasn't binding, the London Convention, in 1985, voted to extend a moratorium on radioactive dumping, and place the "burden of proof" of its safety on nations wanting to empty their witches' cauldrons into international seas.

To speak of any pollution as occurring in "international waters," is, of course, ludicrous. It makes fully as much sense as the old joke about the fisherman who made a mark on the side of his boat so he could find a particularly good fishing spot again the next morning.

Water is no respecter of national boundaries, anymore than fish. What we put into "our" water or air - or "neutral, international" water and air may well end on our dinner tables or in our drinking water - or that of our neighbours in the global village, tomorrow.

No one has yet persuasively determined a "safe" level of radioactive contamination, anymore than we have found a "safe" level of cigarette consumption. All ocean dumping of radioactive wastes should be stopped, until we have methods which are, beyond any respectable argument, utterly safe for our children.

Nuclear wastes reach our oceans from land-based run-off as well. High levels of radioactivity have been found, for example, in North Sea fish. This pollution comes from land-based sources in the United Kingdom and Northwestern Europe. The Paris Convention (the Convention for the Prevention of Marine Pollution from Land-Based Sources) was signed, in 1978, by the European Economic Community and eight other nations. But the Paris Convention says **nothing** about nuclear plants. Moreover the Convention's acceptance of "the best available technology" in determining how much radioactive discharge should be permitted may be lethally ingenuous. It clearly offers few grounds for complacency.

The UN Convention on The Law Of The Sea now has 159 national signatories. It makes each nation clearly responsible for policing its own waters; and it declares forty-five percent of the globe - that part covered by the oceans, to be, "the common heritage of mankind." But as we've observed, most nations are entirely unable to police their own waters. As for our "common heritage," we must accept the fact no one, at the moment, "is minding the shore."

Moreover, several powerful nations have yet to accept the Convention. If it is not ratified by every significant maritime power it will, functionally, become a dead letter. Public disclosure of nations which are dragging their feet on this vital issue should be used to marshall world opinion behind a drive to urge every concerned nation to ratify the Convention. This is the least first step needed to save our seas.

Space, like the seas, is a common and vital shared resource. It is integral to the "market square" or "common" around which our global village is clustered. We have, today, the technology and information to protect our life-saving atmosphere, the "skin" of our global body politic.

We still lack the institutional resources and agreements to use our knowledge.

Our knowledge, like our so-far feeble efforts to protect ourselves and our children, is dispersed, fragmentary and uncoordinated. The United Nations Environment Programme (UNEP) has made modest efforts to pool available space data. It lacks the resources to do enough. Most satellite-gathered information is held, selfishly (and in global survival terms, foolishly) by the national governments collecting those data. Governments must act to share and pool their banks of information.

We've not even, to date, agreed to fairly share the limited number of geosynchronous orbits available over the equator for satellites.

Only in a narrow band over the equator, 36,000 kilometres above the earth, can "stationary" satellites be "parked." As each uses radio communications, they must be widely separated to avoid interference with each other. (This pragmatic consideration limits the maximum number of satellites functioning at any time to 180.)

What's happened, predictably, is an apportioning of the "slots" available to nations with the funds needed to launch and maintain satellites. So the Third World nation states directly under the satellite band have been refused the right even to "reserve" sites for themselves. Their efforts to assert sovereignty in space directly over their national territory have been treated, at best, with amused contempt.

Meanwhile, the industrial nations continue to clutter that crucial, narrow communications highway around the earth's beltline with an astonishing and dangerous array of "space garbage." It ranges from discarded, empty fuel tanks to rocket shells, "dead" satellites, and the shrapnel produced by explosions in space. Most of it could have been avoided with better design and greater care in the disposal of satellites. Today, both the Soviets and the Americans spend tens-of-millions of precious dollars annually simply tracking garbage in space. Every military test in space, by definition, adds to this "littering." As early as 1981, the American Institute of Aeronautics and Astronautics was advised space debris would pose "an unacceptable threat to life in space" within a decade.

(For "life in space" read: the space stations and laboratories we all need and desire - not least for plant and genetic experiments in zero gravity conditions - experiments which hold the promise of crucial advances for us all in medicine, in plant genetics and in resource and energy-efficient industrial processing.)

Nuclear-powered spacecraft are a particularly serious problem. Regulating them is complex and difficult. Banning them by international convention is the simplest and most direct solution. (Because of the heat given off by nuclear power reactors, it would be relatively simple to monitor a moratorium.) Such a ban would, as a side-effect benefiting us all, both economically and in terms of our safety and security, make the development of military space technology impossible. Exceptions to such a ban would likely be appropriate to permit scientific, deep space probes.

Regulation of space debris and of nuclear-powered craft in space is long overdue.

Even more fragile than space, the Antarctic Continent is, we often forget, larger than the combined areas of Mexico and the United States. Its land and adjacent seas are the generators of much of the globe's weather, and the source of nourishment for much of the globe's marine life.

(Though not fully understood, the tiny, shrimp-like 'krill' of Antarctica are believed essential to the world's maritime food chain, up to and including our whales.)

The "Antarctic Treaty," signed December 1, 1959, aims to prohibit all military activity on our southern polar continent, and to promote freedom of scientific study. As well, it bars disposal of any radioactive materials or wastes on the sub-polar cap. At present, only eighteen of the world's nations have full voting status under the terms of the treaty. Again, money is the gatekeeper.

Antarctica is clearly a global resource and needs global protection, yet only those nations with substantial investment in scientific studies and bases on the sub-continent are granted membership in this exclusive club. The rationale, echoing the colonialism of the seventeenth and eighteenth Centuries, is silly. One might equally say those citizens living in nations which can't afford massive power generating stations have no right to complain if their air is poisoned by acid rain.

It's no surprise many developing nations reject the philosophy any of our common, global heritage should be managed by exclusive groups of nations or corporations for their own benefit.

However, the entire world could take a lesson from the experience of Antarctica over the past thirty years.

In this remote part of our global village, at least (and by mutual agreement) there have been no military exercises, no nuclear reactors, no disposal of radioactive waste. Not a bad example for us all.

There's been concern about a "gold rush" to exploit mineral and petroleum resources in the south polar region, with consequently disastrous results for that terribly fragile environment. In a rational world, such fears are groundless. The only minerals found in large enough volume to justify mining - iron in the Prince Charles Mountains, and coal in the Transantarctic Mountains - would cost many kings' ransoms to extract and transport to smelters and markets. We have, beyond that, more of both minerals (in more accessible locales) than we need in the next century, or the one after that.

However, the enthusiasm of minerals exploiters has frequently overstepped the bounds of rationality. The world's nations should take steps to prevent and preclude any minerals exploitation of Antarctica until we have all the data needed to avoid disruption of this vulnerable and essential section of our global village. Such research will almost certainly take at least a generation, even if developed on a "crash basis."

As with the Antarctic, so with the seas and the atmosphere. As usual, Shakespeare had a salutary phrase. Banquo observed, in Macbeth: "The air is delicate."

So are we. The more cause, then, to be robust in our efforts to save our "global commons" and, with them, our children.

Chapter Eleven

THE PROFITS OF WAR VERSUS
THE ENVIRONMENT

Political and military activity have as great a bearing on environmental degradation or survivability as the aggregate impacts of industry, agriculture and all other human enterprise.

At the most basic level, the threat of a nuclear war is the greatest single environmental threat we face. Indeed, to describe it as a "threat" is the understatement of all human history. Even the concepts of environment and development would be swept aside by the probably irreversible consequences of nuclear conflict.

To ignore this caveat to human hope and endeavor would be as witless as it is suicidal. So,

While acknowledging the obvious, that nuclear war would devastate our world, other factors need to be fed into of environmental/development equation:

1. Often, environmental stress has led to military action, rather than the reverse. Nation states, through history, have tended to do whatever-they-felt-necessary to seize or retain the resources they wanted. The desire for gold, oil, sugar, spices, grain, even opium, have all triggered conflict, from Alexander and Tamerlane to Mussolini and Hitler. Even a cursory reading of your daily newspaper will demonstrate the same imperatives at work today, both within and between nations, in Asia, Africa and Latin America.

2. No one could describe mere absence of conflict as a respectable definition of "peace."

Note: Not that we're much used to even "absence-of-conflict." Since the end of World War Two, there've been only forty days during which there was no war raging in some neighbourhood of our global village.

More fundamentally, the notion of "peace" implies we will all be able to concentrate our energies on fruitful development. Well, we've had, at least, no global wars - no direct military confrontation - between the superpowers since 1946.

(Although we have experienced, at incalculable cost, plenty of "surrogate wars" - in Korea, Viet Nam, Angola, Afghanistan, the Middle East, and Latin America.)

So have we reaped the benefits of "peace" in the global sense? You decide, as you consider this sampler of our "peacetime" experience:

- The industrial nations are, today, spending eighteen times more, annually, on military budgets than on foreign aid.

- Reflect on the inflated costs of modern military hardware: if automobile costs had risen as rapidly as those of tanks, planes and missiles, since 1950, a family car would today cost $300,000 U.S.

- By 1984, the world was spending six times more on its military, annually, than the combined total incomes earned by the 3.6 billion people living in all the Third World.

- In 1983, the last year for which we have complete figures, these discrepancies existed:

a) The entire world spent an average of $25,600 to support each soldier and $450 to educate each child. Soldiers, that is, cost us 56.8 times more, each, than school children. **Where were our priorities?**

b) We spent, as a global community, $45 each on military research and $11 each on health research. The machinery of death, that is, had a more than four-to-one priority over the study of life. **Where were our priorities?**

c) Every global citizen, on average, contributed $152 toward military forces, and six cents for peacekeeping. In the period since World War Two, about twenty million people have died in wars - at least two-thirds of those civilians. Yet we spend, still, six cents each, per year, on peacekeeping. **Where are our priorities?**

Not everyone suffers from those "brushfire wars," mind

you. Almost all of them, since 1945, have been fought in the developing world, which thereby bore most of the casualties, and costs. But the bulk of the armaments were made in the West, to the enormous profit of arms-makers and dealers - not least most Western governments:

- From 1964 to 1983, eight industrial nations were the beneficiaries of eighty-five percent of all international arms trade. They were, in descending order, the USSR, the United States, France, the United Kingdom, West Germany, Czechoslovakia, Italy and China. Altogether, $308-billion were spent on arms exports in that period - and two-thirds of all the export trade came from the two superpowers.

In this same twenty-year period, three-quarters of all arms exports were to developing nations - and those arms exports made up half of all "economic development aid" provided to the Third World by the industrial nations. (The U.S. alone has "given" over $50 billion in arms and military training to the Third World since 1946.) **Where were our priorities?**

Every dollar spent on military development in the Third World is a dollar stolen from health services, from education, from the provision of clean drinking water and from rational development. The Bishops of France said, in 1983:

"Every citizen pays the price of . . . armaments - first with taxes - then as a potential victim."

In 1984, UN Secretary-General Javier Perez de Cuellar put the case succinctly:

"The arms trade impoverishes the receiver and debases the supplier. There is a striking resemblance to the drug trade."

Ethics aside (if that is conceivable), military spending clearly distorts both international and national economies, to the profound detriment of development. This theorem is as direct and unanswerable in the industrial world as in developing countries:

In the time between 1960 and 1983, as a case in point, there was a direct and inverse relation, in industrial nations, between their spending on arms and their manufacturing productivity. Some examples:

Country	Increase in Arms Spending	Increase in IndustrialGrowth
Japan	1 %	9 %
Canada	3 %	3.5 %
U.S.	7 %	2.5 %
USSR	11 %	3 %

While industrial nations were increasing their military spending by eighty percent, from 1960 to 1983 (after allowing for inflation), their spending on foreign aid actually dropped in real terms, from $8.50 per Third World resident to $8.40. The largest share of aid, moreover, went to "middle income" developing nations - those with a stake in military alliances tied to the superpowers.

One final example of the distortions in development planning caused by arms spending:

In 1982, average military spending, per soldier, was $9,810 in the developing nations. Average yearly educational spending, in these same countries was $91 per school child. The investment in each soldier was, in other words, 107.8 times more than the amount spent to educate each child. **Where were our priorities?**

It can scarcely be a complete coincidence, either, that some of the world's most impoverished areas environmentally have also seen severe political/military disruption. Among these are Ethiopia, where the drought and famine of the early Seventies was caused as much by unsound land use as changing weather; Haiti, where one-sixth of the entire population has fled an island plagued by some of world's most severe erosion; El Salvador - again with the worst and most extensive soil erosion in its region. In many locales, the roots of political conflict are found in the destruction of the environmental base. Impoverished populations, desperate for arable land and food, do not make for stable nations.

(In 1984/85 alone, the globe had fifteen million refugees - a majority of them "environmental refugees," driven from their land and homes by drought or flood, by hunger and loss of income. Ten million of these were in Africa. Their migrations have created enormous political strains, not least

112

when they cross national boundaries and find themselves in competition with the almost equally poor residents of neighbouring states for food, shelter, social services and jobs.)

In a classic example of how the vicious circle of both environmental degradation and political strain - even armed conflict, can be started, witness the apartheid policies of South Africa. The equation for civil strife is clear and seemingly irreversible under present government policies:

-      The government's "homelands" policy has provided just fourteen percent of South Africa's land to the black seventy-two percent of her population.

-      Working-age black Africans flee those over-cultivated and over-grazed areas to find work and food in the cities.

-      These environmental migrants add to the crowding and squalor of black, urban "townships," where they mostly find scant economic opportunity.

-      Tensions rise, repression escalates; its victims often seek sanctuary across the nearest national borders, and justice - or revenge - from those sanctuaries. The South African regime retaliates with cross-border raids; and the armed conflict widens into the so-called "Front Line States" surrounding South Africa. One can only hope the events of 1990 presage a fundamental change.

Environment-based disputes are more common than we generally suppose. Eighty of our national, global neighbours already suffer acute water shortages. Major disputes over river water are common. We experienced them:

-      In North America: over the Rio Grande.

-      In South America: over the Rio de la Plata and the Parana Rivers.

-      In South and Southeast Asia: over the waters of the Ganges and the Mekong.

-      In Africa: where the waters of the Nile are in dispute, and,

-      In the Middle East: the Jordan, the Litani, the Orontes and the Euphrates Rivers have all been fought over.

Fisheries, too, are creating tensions as stocks dwindle:

The Iceland/United Kingdom "cod war" of 1974 was no aberration. Similar tensions exist today in both the Japanese and Korean Seas and on both sides of the South

Atlantic. Despite the restoration of diplomatic exchanges, future relations between Britain and Argentina have been strained even further by the declaration of "an exclusive fishing zone," in disputed waters around the Malvinas/Falkland Islands.

Tomorrow's anxieties for adequate resources will almost certainly be exacerbated, too, by the "greenhouse" effect of global warming trends, caused by atmospheric build-up of carbon dioxide et al. Climatic changes of the order envisaged would certainly disrupt a large part of the world's cereal harvests, and would likely trigger mass migration in areas already hard-hit by hunger.

Looming over all these threats, still, is the global arms race. In Dwight D. Eisenhower's words, as he retired from the U.S. presidency:

"Every gun that is made, every warship launched, every rocket fired, represents, in the final analysis, a theft from those who are cold and are not clothed."

Today, a half-million scientists are employed, globally, on military research. Half of all research and development effort in the world goes to inventing new weapons systems. Call that $80 billion in 1984 alone. **Where are our priorities?**

A few nations - Peru, Argentina and China among them - have demonstrated how nations can shift spending from military to development priorities without disrupting their economies. The rest of us have still to learn this vital lesson.

In the developing world, besides eating huge fractions of national budgets desperately needed for social and economic development, military spending (which has increased fivefold in twenty years) uses precious "hard currency" for equipment, parts, replacements and training. In this regard, the industrial states - formerly colonial powers - resemble a "fire brigade" busy starting fires to keep themselves employed. Examples:

a) There are, today, forty border disputes in the Third World. They were caused chiefly by ill-defined and arbitrarily-imposed national boundaries drawn by the colonial nations; those borders were often organized to "divide-and-pacify," to give political balances-of-power to "friendly" tribal groups or cultures, or to ensure easy access to raw resources.

(All these disputes, naturally, allow the industrial nations to fatten their purses with arms sales for the "security" of their client states in the Third World - a case of "mercenary fire-fighting" globally.)

b) The industrial states and superpowers have frequently and blatantly used Third World disputes as areas of surrogate conflict, as observed earlier, and at little cost to themselves. These "test beds" for new weaponry and tactics (one is reminded of Hitler's "Condor Legion" in the Spanish Civil War, over fifty years ago) seem, frequently, to be at least "fanned," if not actually created, for the selfish, equally short-sighted, political and military purposes of the superpowers.

We are, as neighbours in this small, global village, past the time when we must recognize **there are no military solutions to environmental hardship.** World cooperation is our only hope; dedication to developmental research and environmentally-sound growth our only salvation. **There are no solutions, for any of us, at the end of a gun barrel.**

Consider the alternatives, based on 1985's world arms costs of well over $900 billion - more than $2.5 billion daily:

- Twelve hours of military spending, over five years, would repair the globe's tropical rain forests, insofar as that is possible.

- Forty-three hours of arms costs, each year for the next twenty years, would roll-back the appalling waste caused by the global advance of the deserts destroying our croplands.

- The UN plan to provide safe water for everyone on earth would reduce Third World disease by eighty percent. That incredible change would use up merely ten days' military costs per year, for ten years.

- It would cost us an extra nine hours' worth of defence costs, every year, to make family planning information and birth control devices freely available to every woman in the developing nations.

- Throw in another fourteen-or-so hours' spending to immunize all the children of the Third World - where one child died, today, every six seconds (five million dead this year), for want of vaccination.

Make that a grand total of thirteen days and six hours' "human investment" stolen from military hardware, training and research spending, to save maybe twenty million lives each year, and to protect and restore more farmlands than the combined areas of Europe and India over the next twenty years.

Put it another way:

To achieve those spending levels on life, instead of the machinery of death, we would have to reduce global arms costs by 3.6 percent. Is the price too high? **Where are our priorities?**

"Military economists" (if the terms are not mutually exclusive) are fond of computing and announcing 'body counts," and, in terms of "efficient military technology," the ratios of "bang-for-the-buck."   So how have we done on this battered globe, as we have quadrupled military spending, and stockpiled enough nuclear weapons to destroy each of us, twelve times over? This well:

-     In the period between World War One and World War Two, there were eighty-three armed conflicts around the world. In the time since World War Two, we have had 120 wars.

-     Since World War Two, four times as many have died in wars as in the comparative period before 1939. Two-thirds of these, at least, have been civilians - largely women and children.

You say. It is your world, after all, and your children's. How are we doing? Your voice should be heard.

When we gather in our international assemblies; when we speak to our political leaders, directly or through the ballot box; when we answer pollsters' questions; when we tell our children and grandchildren "what the future holds for them":

Where are your priorities?

Chapter Twelve

PRESERVING OUR WORLD

The greatest paradox of our time lies in the surging tide of Western protectionism and isolation; this precisely when we most need vastly to increase the mechanisms of global cooperation and build bridges of mutual trust.

All the world, including the industrial West, suffers from soil erosion, desertification and deforestation in the Third World; nor are the developed nations armoured against the loss of tropical rain forests and of plant and animal species. All the world, including the developing nations, shares the risks created by acid rain, by the greenhouse effect, by the wanton distribution and dumping of toxic chemicals and wastes: none of us is immune to the consequences of resource depletion, energy waste, industrial pollution - or of nuclear conflict. There is an appropriate biblical proscription, in Galatians, chapter six, verse seven:

"Be not deceived; God is not mocked: for whatsoever a man soweth, that shall he also reap."

The warning is easily transposed to any culture, any religion:

"Be not deceived; nature is not mocked."

Whether, as individuals in the global village, we see in the fragile unity of planetary life the hand of God (or gods), or the balance of nature, our conclusions must agree:

Ignorant or careless tampering with the world's natural checks-and-balances can no more be countenanced.

We know, too, from our demonstrations-of-failure, the "quick fix" approach to the riddles and ravages of threats to environmentally-sound development is both naive and futile. With the world under siege, we must settle ourselves to working with long and difficult remedies.

We've seen how the old approaches to developmental and environmental security have only increased instability. We can find safety only through change. We're embarked, if you will, on an existential trip into the future.

We'll learn as we go, from our journey, or we'll have nowhere left to go.

It's the journey itself which holds the promise of human survival and hope.

Today, most agencies concerned with environment and development are paying exclusive attention to "effects." They are still "reactive" not "proactive." It's time to concern ourselves with the diseases rather than the symptoms. It's the sources of those effects we must identify and eliminate.

The global village will find most of its task, and its challenge, written "between the lines" of our experience and institutions:

We know national boundaries, confronted by the global migrations of pollution in our air and water, are as porous as fish nets. There are gaps as real and dangerous in our international law, our trade treaties, our economic development schemes and aid policies. We've got to fill those gaps and strengthen the laws - the tools and institutions of our mutual survival.

We are going to have more and bigger crises. Their origins are in our recent history of ignorance and carelessness, their gestation long past, their arrival unavoidable. So we must cooperate, first, in risk assessment and crisis management.

To ensure development we can live with, we must invest in our future by making informed choices, and back them with the legal and fiscal muscle needed to assess the risks, identify the diseases - and end them, while still treating their symptoms. Some essential steps to those ends:

- Governments must report annually - and publicly, on their environmental resources, and their "audit" of changes in them.

- Every department, agency, and activity of government must be held publicly accountable for building the needs of sound environmental protection into every programme.

- Every government should adopt a universally accepted "environmental foreign policy." We have to stop exporting degradation, disease and death - even "by default."

- Many new bilateral and multi-lateral agreements will be needed to resolve regional and sub-regional problems of

118

cross-border pollution - not least in the world's great river basins. (Fewer than thirty of the globe's two hundred major, international river basins are now safeguarded by formal, cooperative protection.)

- The United Nations must be made the centre and focus of international cooperation. Efforts to ensure healthy, continuing development - and just distribution of the world's resources and opportunities - must be multiplied.

- Every UN agency should re-deploy appropriate staff and funds to make environmental priorities central to their every activity.

- National governments must make a major effort to supply the resources and support the UN will need during the critical twenty years ahead.

- The United Nations Secretary General should appoint a special UN board or commission (under his/her chairmanship) to monitor and encourage "sustainable development." This board would oversee and encourage the actions of United Nations agencies and organizations. It would also provide a "hinge" or liaison with national governments and with other world bodies. It would stay in direct and regular communication with a further new group:

- A "risk assessment" centre, headed by a steering committee composed of internationally eminent individuals. This risk assessment commission would coordinate and encourage the efforts especially of non-governmental organizations, both national and international. It would also establish centres of excellence drawing on world authorities in such areas as law, economics and science - with those recruited for these tasks "on call" to advise any agency calling on them for help.

- The United Nations Environment Programme (UNEP) will need an infusion of larger and more reliable funding along with the overt support of UN member nations. UNEP should be equipped to:

a) Monitor, assess and report on global environment (through its "Earthwatch" programme).

b) Encourage international agreements, and promote the extension of current pacts and treaties: this while developing patterns for future accord in such areas as that of international river basins and the disposal of hazardous wastes.

c) Support the development of expertise and of regulatory and monitoring capacities in developing nations.

d) Provide the major global centre of data and reporting on all environmental matters.

e) Advise and assist UN organizations and agencies (not excluding the World Bank) and offer training schemes and technical assistance to personnel of these agencies.

The globe's risk assessment programme should be centred in UNEP. As the major repository of environmental data, it will be the only logical locus for study-of and extrapolation-from those data.

Urgent steps must be taken to provide global access to the monitoring and analysis of our ecosphere now undertaken, in a fragmented way, by many individual nations and agencies. This information is vital to our global village; shared, it will multiply in value.

Non-governmental organizations will need far more support, in three forms:

a) More money.

b) More information: they must be kept aware of new policies, proposals, projects.

c) More consultation: they have enormous on-the-ground expertise; they should be consulted at the planning stages of any project likely to have environmental impact. (They also have a very broad constituency-of-support which can be marshalled - only by them - in support of protection of our global commons.)

Beyond the foregoing, these NGOs must begin to exchange more information between themselves. Too often in the past they have seen themselves as competitors for very small portions of globally-available funds for development. We must find and encourage systems to help them become much more mutually supportive and, thereby, effective.

The public's "right to know" must be reinforced and actively pursued, in international agencies as well as within national governmental or private organizations. This means, not least:

a) The right to informed consultation, and a recognized

role in decision-making.

b) The right to legal redress and remedy for anyone whose health or environment is effected by the acts of others - be they governments or corporations. Our resources of minerals, water, air, our flora and fauna, have no access to "class action" legislation in their own defence. So we must, as individuals, assume those rights, and undertake the consequent responsibilities.

An active and urgent follow-up to the findings of the Brundtland Report is imperative. To that end:

a) The UN General Assembly, after full consideration of this report, should move from that study to development of a United Nations "action programme" on sustainable development.

b) The United Nations General Assembly should develop and adopt a "universal declaration" on environment and development similar to its Declaration of Human Rights. This statement of principle should, as quickly as possible, be then converted into an international convention; every UN member state should be urged to sign and abide by that convention.

c) National governments must be pressed to ratify and promote existing international and regional conventions and treaties dealing with environment and development. As critically, each government must apply the principles of those treaties with dedication, discipline and rigour. The best-intended agreements are merely pious declarations until they are translated into active, living codes of behaviour.

d) Effectual conciliation of international and bilateral environmental disputes is integral to progress in our global village. Where nations cannot reach agreement within a reasonable time - eighteen months should be the maximum, given the globe's quickening pace of ecosystem degradation - disputes should be submitted to conciliation procedures (at the request of any party to the disagreement). If still unresolved, the matter should proceed to compulsory arbitration or judicial disposition.

"Binding settlements" are not the ideal means of achieving international agreement. But the clock is running out on our environment. We need the means to speed agreements - not

121

least by encouraging concerned parties to resolve their problems by mutual consent, rather than at the hands of an arbitrator.

The World Court is a considerably under-used resource in this area. Moreover, the Court has declared its willingness and capacity to deal with cases in this area, fully and promptly. The Court's readiness will be of little use, however, if nations continue to perceive its findings as "binding" only when in their favour, and "irrelevant" when on the opposite side.

e) National governments should instruct their representatives on all regional and international bodies (such as the World Bank, for example) to make environment priorities an integral part of every policy and programme decision.

This applies, in the broadest sense, as much to trade and tariff negotiations at GATT (the General Agreement on Tariffs and Trade) or at disarmament talks between the superpowers, as elsewhere.

The aid agencies of the industrial nations - the so-called "bilateral aid agencies" offering help from one nation state to another - now provide four times more aid to the developing world than all of the international agencies (such as the UN) combined. Without the enthusiastic support and participation of these national agencies, no plan to tie development to sensible environmental protection is possible. So consider this:

A 1980 survey of six major, national aid agencies showed just one, US A.I.D., had both systematic concerns in this area and adequate staff to monitor and police those concerns. In the years since, several other nations have made "policy" progress. They have developed "guidelines," even increased funding for some specific environmental projects. But our check of those new guidelines found almost no evidence they were being systematically applied. More paper tigers. The world - the environment - needs substance, not appearance. The harsh truth is this:

Most funding for international environmental action in our lifetimes has come through individual, voluntary contributions - with the bulk of those channeled through the

NGOs - the non-governmental organizations. National governments and aid agencies **must by persuaded, not least by marshalling public opinion, to join this effort.**

g) New and secure funding sources must be found to sustain the effort needed. The United Nations General Assembly should seriously consider some of the alternate financing ideas suggested by a number of studies. So should all national governments. Possible sources of new money include:

i) Some form of "royalty," "license fee" or "lease agreement" with corporations and nations using the space and resources we all share - the elements of our "global common." Examples:
- Ocean fishing.
- Ocean transport.
- Sea-bed mining.
- "Parking fees" for geostationary satellites.
- "Leases" for scientific bases in Antarctica.

ii) Taxes levied on international trade, not excluding the "invisible exports" of services, technical expertise and investment. Such taxes could be considered, alternatively or additionally, on trade surpluses, or on "luxury goods." Trade in finite and diminishing resources - especially in endangered species - would presumably be taxed very highly, where such trade is permitted at all.

Our global village is not going to be saved by some philanthropic space creature, arriving from a distant galaxy, in a flying saucer crammed with panaceas for all our ills.

Our help is within us.

Our strength is between us.

Our need is as fundamental as our life support systems of air to breathe, water to drink, food to eat. It is our air, food and water.

Our responsibility is to our human seed. They will neither grow nor prosper unless we prepare, today, for their needs.

If we fail we need fear no recriminations from history. There may well be no one left to write the histories of our impotence.

If we begin to succeed, historians may remember this

generation as the one which started to turn Earth back, toward Eden.

Chapter Thirteen

WHAT WE CAN DO
The Challenge of the Brundtland Report

Madame Gro Harlem Brundtland coined the phrase to explain what's required from each of us, if we are to preserve our world:
"Think globally - act locally."
We must, in short, consider all of the planet and its people - and their future - in our individual, daily activities. That's getting easier all the time:

There are now several books available to explain how we can shop for environmentally friendly products. Many nations have developed logos and labels to help us indentify consumer goods which do not damage our planet. Other publications tell us how to conserve energy, how to reduce our waste of water and fuel, how to avoid fouling our gardens with poisonous chemicals.

Each of us can have a major impact on our global village by observing the four "R" rules of planetary restoration:

> **Reduce**
> **Re-use**
> **Recycle**
> **Reject**

To explain:

-    We must all **reduce** waste of our resources. That means cutting down on useless packaging (carry your own shopping bag instead of accumulating useless plastic ones), walking or cycling short distances instead of driving, using a cloth to mop-up spills instead of a paper towel

-    It's time we began practicing frugality with our small world by **re-using** products instead of adding them to our mountains of polluting garbage. Automobile motor oil and anti-freeze can be re-used; so can cleaning cloths, ordinary envelopes (with a new address label), re-chargeable batteries and cloth diapers.

- We can **recycle** a huge volume of our "garbage," as is done throughout the developing world. That applies to glass, paper, metals, plastics, even chemicals. It applies at home, too, where we can use the back of used sheets of paper as scratch pads, turn tattered bedsheets into cleaning cloths, pass children's clothing on to a friend or relative, even compost our organic garbage to grow next year's vegetables and flowers.

- We can also **reject** goods and services which damage our world. Begin with aerosol containers, products containing CFCs, any over-packaged products and just about every throw-away, disposal item in the shops - from razors and cigarette lighters to cameras and plastic shower caps.

An entire book can be written on each of these areas. But awareness is the beginning of our salvation. You'll have no trouble finding and following a thousand examples of each. Remember, though, that the services we all "buy" include those of government at every level. So scrutinize those "services," too:

In most of the world, about fifty per cent of all money spent ends in the hands of government. As government's clients and customers, we are well-entitled to demand environmentally-responsible policies and practices.

In almost every country - and every sizeable community - there are many organizations dedicated to environmental goals, and to monitoring and lobbying government. Join one - or several - and share their impact on public policy. If there's no group pursuing goals you see as vital, start one. Begin with a few friends or neighbours. Individuals, working together, can move mountains of inertia and create miracles of conservation and restoration.

Look at what's happening in the schools in your community, and at your workplace: Is there a recycling programme? Have disposable products (e.g. polystyrene coffee cups) been replaced with re-usable, non-polluting items (crockery mugs, for example)?

Support businesses which are helping the environment. Ask your dry cleaner or photo-developer if they recycle their chemicals. Ask your mechanic if your motor oil and anti-freeze are being recycled. Ask your grocers if they bale and recycle their cardboard cartons. Ask your newspaper publishers if they buy recycled newsprint. Ask your pharmacists if they will take back used, plastic pill bottles and clean and re-use them.

With the planet at stake, it would be hard to imagine any gesture too small to be of importance. American journalist Edward R. Murrow spoke for our environment in the Forties when he said:

"If we do not take care of the present, the future will take its revenge."

Study the recommendations of the Brundtland Report. Talk about them with your children, your friends, your colleagues at work, your politicians. Consider them individually - and think about how each can be implemented in your home, in your office, in your club or community organization, in your school, in your neighbourhood, in your city - in your life.

Maybe we can paraphrase the "golden rule" just a little, for the sake of our children, and theirs:

"Do unto the environment as you would have it do unto you."

We don't own the planet and its resources. We merely hold them in trust for future generations.

All the great philosophers tell us life without purpose is meaningless. What more noble purpose, what greater meaning to life that the goal of "preserving our world"?

Even better, as we can learn from Madame Brundtland, this is no "fountain of youth" or Utopia we seek. This goal - with dedication, with concerted effort, with the political will created by public demand, **with sustainable development** - is attainable.

Failure would be unthinkable.

So plant a tree. Help create a new park, or clean up an old one. Sweep your pavement instead of wasting water to clean it. Begin to treat the environment molesters with the contempt they deserve. Stop accepting political rhetoric in place of action. Get involved in the biggest recycling programme of them all:

Join those who are busy dusting and cleaning our planet and making certain no one walks on it without cleaning their boots, or drops garbage on our carpet. When we're through we can wrap the global village in a festive (and re-usable!) ribbon and present our children with the one gift no money can buy:

A safe and healthy future.

What could be better?

A WORD ABOUT
"THE WORLD COMMISION ON ENVIRONMENT
AND DEVELOPMENT"
(which produced the WCED or "Brundtland" Report,
titled, "Our Common Future")

In December, 1983, responding to a UN General Assembly Declaration, United Nations Secretary-General Perez de Cuellar appointed Madame Gro Harlem Brundtland as Chairman of an independent commission to examine our global economy and development in the harsh light of environmental concern. What a choice she was!

A graduate of the Harvard School of Medicine, former Public Health Officer of Oslo and currently Prime Minister of Norway, Gro Brundtland was a dedicated humanist and environmentalist, a politician with a clear global perspective, a pragmatist and a demonstrably brilliant arbitrator and administrator. And what a team of commissioners she recruited!

They were from Norway, Sudan, Italy, Saudi Arabia, Mexico, Zimbabwe, Ivory Coast, the Federal Republic of Germany, Hungary, China, Columbia, the Netherlands, Brazil, Japan, the U.S., the UK, Indonesia, Nigeria, the USSR, Yugoslavia and Canada.

The miracle was that this disparate group, which began composing their report, in a Moscow hotel room in December, 1986, produced a unanimous report in April, 1987. That WCED Report, describing how, "**people may build a future that is more prosperous, more just and more secure..**" may well be seen, if we save our global village, as the landmark document of the Twentieth Century.

ABOUT "THE CENTRE FOR
OUR COMMON FUTURE" IN GENEVA

As you may have noted on the back cover of this book, the author and publishers are sharing their income from all book sales with the Centre.

Launched in April, 1988, one year after publication of the WCED Report, The Centre has become a clearing house, data base, point-of-contact and source of inspiration for every citizen in the global village monitoring response to the Brundtland Report.

The newsletter published by the Centre is required reading for any journalist, politician, environmentalist who cares about 'our common future'. The Executive Director of The Centre, Warren H. (Chip) Linder has moved with grace and stunning energy and impact from his work with the WCED to the new Centre.

Funding for the Centre and its activities is appallingly limited. That's why, after canvassing all the environmental causes to which we might send some small token of support from sales of this book, we selected The Centre without pause or hesitation.

Please remember the brilliant definitions of Gro Brundtland: (Genius, of course, lies always in noting the obvious - when no one else has managed to do that!)

" The environment is where we all live. Development is what we all do."

We are all, that is, and by defintion, environmentalists, if we care for the survival of our planet and our children. To that end - and for your own sake - may I urge you to subscribe to the newsletter published by The Centre For Our Common Future. The address:

Palais Wilson, 52 rue des Paquis,
CH-1201, Geneva, Switzerland

ABOUT THE AUTHOR

A veteran journalist, Troyer has conducted more than 10,000 radio and television interviews, written seven best selling books published in six languages, written/directed/produced more than 600 documentary films. He has worked as a daily newspaper and magazine editor, radio and tv producer and director, public speaker, communications consultant, university teacher, syndicated columnist, magazine writer, etc., etc.

Troyer's environmental concerns date back to freelance radio features and newspaper articles in 1952-'54, his first documentary, in 1956, and his first book, "No Safe Place", in 1976.

He has, as a print and tv correspondent, covered events on every major continent concentrating on political, military and social affairs. He worked, for five years, in Asia and Africa, both on foreign aid projects in communications, and in production of UNICEF-sponsored documentary films. He has taught in several universities and worked as a communications consultant for the United Nations, several governments and a host of international organizations from the Red Cross to the World Council of Churches.

Troyer has won numerous Canadian and international awards as a writer, editor, film director and producer.